THE Matthew
Challenge

Unless otherwise noted, all Scripture quotations are from the World English Bible (WEB), published 2000, public domain.

ISBN: 978-1-950791-20-0

Cover and text layout design: Kristi Yoder

Printed in the USA

Published by:
TGS International
P.O. Box 355
Berlin, Ohio 44610 USA
Phone: 330.893.4828
Fax: 330.893.2305
www.tgsinternational.com

THE Matthew
Challenge

Discover who Jesus is in 28 days

Lester Bauman

Introduction

The first four books of the New Testament are called Gospels. All four tell the story of Jesus from a different perspective and to a different audience. Matthew's Gospel was written especially to the Jews, to show them that Jesus was a King and had the right to be a King. Matthew also gives us an onlooker's perspective of the life and deeds of the greatest person who ever lived.

Our billboard ministry has a practice of encouraging people who want to know more about Jesus to do the "Matthew challenge." This involves studying one chapter of the Gospel of

Matthew each day for 28 days, and writing down some of your insights.

To benefit from this book and the Matthew challenge, you need to carefully read the chapter of Matthew designated for each day. Each day's chapter is included in this book to make it easier for you to do this. This book will help to guide your thinking, but as you read the chapter ask God to guide your thoughts as well.

Don't rush your reading. Take time to think about what each day's passage shows you about Jesus. As you think of titles or adjectives that describe Jesus in the passage you are reading, write them down. You can do this in your own notebook or in the section provided in the back of this book. If you do this, by the time you finish reading the book you will have your own personal list that answers the question, **Who Is Jesus?**

DAY 1

Who Is Jesus?

For unto us a child is born. . . . And His name will be
called Wonderful, Counselor, Mighty God, Everlasting
Father, Prince of Peace. Isaiah 9:6, NKJV

READ MATTHEW 1

The Genealogy of Jesus Christ

[1] The book of the genealogy of Jesus Christ, the son of David, the son of Abraham.

[2] Abraham became the father of Isaac. Isaac became the father of Jacob. Jacob became the father of Judah and his brothers.

[3] Judah became the father of Perez and Zerah by Tamar. Perez became the father of Hezron. Hezron became the father of Ram.

[4] Ram became the father of Amminadab. Amminadab became the father of Nahshon. Nahshon became the father of Salmon.

[5] Salmon became the father of Boaz by Rahab. Boaz became the father of Obed

by Ruth. Obed became the father of Jesse.

⁶ Jesse became the father of King David. David became the father of Solomon by her who had been Uriah's wife.

⁷ Solomon became the father of Rehoboam. Rehoboam became the father of Abijah. Abijah became the father of Asa.

⁸ Asa became the father of Jehoshaphat. Jehoshaphat became the father of Joram. Joram became the father of Uzziah.

⁹ Uzziah became the father of Jotham. Jotham became the father of Ahaz. Ahaz became the father of Hezekiah.

¹⁰ Hezekiah became the father of Manasseh. Manasseh became the father of Amon. Amon became the father of Josiah.

¹¹ Josiah became the father of Jechoniah and his brothers, at the time of the exile to Babylon.

¹² After the exile to Babylon, Jechoniah became the father of Shealtiel. Shealtiel became the father of Zerubbabel.

¹³ Zerubbabel became the father of Abiud. Abiud became the father of Eliakim. Eliakim became the father of Azor.

¹⁴ Azor became the father of Zadok. Zadok became the father of Achim. Achim became the father of Eliud.

¹⁵ Eliud became the father of Eleazar. Eleazar became the father of Matthan. Matthan became the father of Jacob.

¹⁶ Jacob became the father of Joseph, the husband of Mary, from whom was born Jesus, who is called Christ.

¹⁷ So all the generations from Abraham to David are fourteen generations; from David to the exile to Babylon fourteen generations; and from the carrying away to Babylon to the Christ, fourteen generations.

The Birth of Jesus Christ

¹⁸ Now the birth of Jesus Christ was like this: After his mother, Mary, was engaged to Joseph, before they came together, she was found pregnant by the Holy Spirit.

¹⁹ Joseph, her husband, being a righteous man, and not willing to make her a public example, intended to put her away secretly.

^{20} But when he thought about these things, behold, an angel of the Lord appeared to him in a dream, saying, "Joseph, son of David, don't be afraid to take to yourself Mary, your wife, for that which is conceived in her is of the Holy Spirit.

^{21} She shall give birth to a son. You shall call his name Jesus, for it is he who shall save his people from their sins."

^{22} Now all this has happened, that it might be fulfilled which was spoken by the Lord through the prophet, saying,

^{23} "Behold, the virgin shall be with child, and shall give birth to a son. They shall call his name Immanuel;" which is, being interpreted, "God with us."

^{24} Joseph arose from his sleep, and did as the angel of the Lord commanded him, and took his wife to himself;

^{25} and didn't know her sexually until she had given birth to her firstborn son. He named him Jesus.

Introduction

The Jews placed a lot of emphasis on genealogy. The offices of priest or Levite could be filled only by men who could trace their bloodline back to the right person. Matthew, therefore, starts with Jesus' ancestry. He shows that Jesus was born into a family that could be traced back to King David, thus giving Him the right to claim kingship as a man.

Who Is Jesus?

Jesus was often accused of being an illegitimate child, so it is easy to understand why Matthew addressed this question in the first chapter of his Gospel.

The conception of Jesus was a miracle. Anyone believing the truth about His birth realizes that He was no ordinary person!

Think of all the extraordinary circumstances . . .

- An angel announced His birth.
- Prophets foretold His birth hundreds of years before it occurred.
- God was His Father and a human virgin was His mother.

Joseph and Mary, as well as the other people who knew the truth about this, gave it a lot of thought. It is a good thing for us to think about as well.

So who was Jesus? We can summarize it as follows:

- Jesus had a human mother, so He was a **man**.
- Jesus' family came from a royal bloodline, so He was a **King**.
- Jesus was conceived by the power of the Holy Spirit, so He was also the **Son of God**.

This gave Him the right to claim divinity, kingship, and humanity. Jesus was the only person ever born who could meet all three of these criteria. Most importantly, He was the only man ever born who was also God.

To Think About

1. Jesus' miraculous conception put Mary in a very difficult position. Many people no doubt considered her story ridiculous. How would you have felt if you had been in Mary's place? Or Joseph's?

2. Can you think of some ways that a person who was both God and man would be different from a normal person?

3. What was the main reason for Jesus' birth, according to the angel in Joseph's dream?

Thank you, Lord, for sending your Son to live on earth to save me from my sins.

JESUS IS ... a King
who is both God
and man.

DAY 2

Who Is Jesus?

For unto us a child is born. . . . Of the increase of his
government and peace there shall be no end, upon the
throne of David and over his kingdom, to order it and
establish it with judgment and justice from that time
forward, even forever. Isaiah 9:6–7, NKJV

READ MATTHEW 2

The Visit of the Wise Men

¹ Now when Jesus was born in Bethlehem of Judea in the days of King Herod, behold, wise men from the east came to Jerusalem, saying,

² "Where is he who is born King of the Jews? For we saw his star in the east, and have come to worship him."

³ When King Herod heard it, he was troubled, and all Jerusalem with him.

⁴ Gathering together all the chief priests and scribes of the people, he asked them where the Christ would be born.

⁵ They said to him, "In Bethlehem of Judea, for this is written through the prophet,

⁶ 'You Bethlehem, land of Judah, are in no way least among the princes of Judah: for out of you shall come a governor, who shall shepherd my people, Israel.' "

⁷ Then Herod secretly called the wise men, and learned from them exactly what time the star appeared.

⁸ He sent them to Bethlehem, and said, "Go and search diligently for the young child. When you have found him, bring me word, so that I also may come and worship him."

⁹ They, having heard the king, went their way; and behold, the star, which they saw in the east, went before them, until it came and stood over where the young child was.

¹⁰ When they saw the star, they rejoiced with exceedingly great joy.

¹¹ They came into the house and saw the young child with Mary, his mother, and they fell down and worshiped him. Opening their treasures, they offered to him gifts: gold, frankincense, and myrrh.

¹² Being warned in a dream not to return to Herod, they went back to their own country another way.

The Flight to Egypt

¹³ Now when they had departed, behold, an angel of the Lord appeared to Joseph in a dream, saying, "Arise and take the young child and his mother, and flee into Egypt, and stay there until I tell you, for Herod will seek the young child to destroy him."

¹⁴ He arose and took the young child and his mother by night, and departed into Egypt,

¹⁵ and was there until the death of Herod; that it might be fulfilled which was spoken by the Lord through the prophet, saying, "Out of Egypt I called my son."

Herod Kills the Children

¹⁶ Then Herod, when he saw that he was mocked by the wise men, was exceedingly angry, and sent out, and killed all the male children who were in Bethlehem and in all the surrounding countryside, from two years old and under, according to the exact time which he had learned from the wise men.

¹⁷ Then that which was spoken by Jeremiah the prophet was fulfilled, saying,

¹⁸ "A voice was heard in Ramah, lamentation, weeping and great mourning, Rachel weeping for her children; she wouldn't be comforted, because they are no more."

The Return to Nazareth

[19] But when Herod was dead, behold, an angel of the Lord appeared in a dream to Joseph in Egypt, saying,

[20] "Arise and take the young child and his mother, and go into the land of Israel, for those who sought the young child's life are dead."

[21] He arose and took the young child and his mother, and came into the land of Israel.

[22] But when he heard that Archelaus was reigning over Judea in the place of his father, Herod, he was afraid to go there. Being warned in a dream, he withdrew into the region of Galilee,

[23] and came and lived in a city called Nazareth; that it might be fulfilled which was spoken through the prophets: "He will be called a Nazarene."

Who Is Jesus?

Several Old Testament prophets wrote that a king would be born someday who would lead God's people. In this chapter, Matthew focuses on the fact that Jesus fulfilled these Old Testament prophecies.

The wise men from the East recognized Jesus as a King. But He was not just an ordinary king. God had announced His birth by a special sign in the skies. These men had spent time studying these things, and they recognized the meaning of the unusual star they saw. This was a King worthy of their worship. But they didn't know where to find Him. So they went to Jerusalem, a religious center, hoping to find out.

Herod recognized from the description the wise men gave that this could be "the Christ." Through Biblical prophecy, the religious rulers identified his birthplace. Herod wasn't worried about the Biblical side of it; he was more concerned about a possible threat to his rule. Whether the baby was a god or a man, or both, he decided to take no chances and try to get rid of Him.

Jesus was born where the prophet said He would be, enabling the wise men to find Him and worship Him. Matthew uses this story to strengthen his point that Jesus was a King.

To Think About

1. The wise men were probably Gentiles, yet they understood who Jesus was and why He came. Why might they have gone to such great effort to recognize Him when God's own people paid so little attention?

2. Notice all the fulfilled prophecies that Matthew pointed out in this chapter. Why do you think he did this?

3. God gave His Son into the care of a human family. Jesus was raised like any other child. God didn't pamper His Son. Can you think of some possible reasons that God placed His Son into a poor, working-class home, rather than into the home of a rich man or a king?

Thank you, Father, for giving us your Son to be our King.

JESUS IS ... a King
with a human background.

DAY 3

Who Is Jesus?

The voice of one crying in the wilderness: Prepare
the way of the Lord; make straight in the desert a
highway for our God. Isaiah 40:3, NKJV

READ MATTHEW 3

John the Baptist Prepares the Way

[1] In those days, John the Baptizer came, preaching in the wilderness of
Judea, saying,

[2] "Repent, for the Kingdom of Heaven is at hand!"

[3] For this is he who was spoken of by Isaiah the prophet, saying, "The voice
of one crying in the wilderness, make ready the way of the Lord. Make his
paths straight."

[4] Now John himself wore clothing made of camel's hair, with a leather belt
around his waist. His food was locusts and wild honey.

⁵ Then people from Jerusalem, all of Judea, and all the region around the Jordan went out to him.

⁶ They were baptized by him in the Jordan, confessing their sins.

⁷ But when he saw many of the Pharisees and Sadducees coming for his baptism, he said to them, "You offspring of vipers, who warned you to flee from the wrath to come?

⁸ Therefore produce fruit worthy of repentance!

⁹ Don't think to yourselves, 'We have Abraham for our father,' for I tell you that God is able to raise up children to Abraham from these stones.

¹⁰ "Even now the ax lies at the root of the trees. Therefore every tree that doesn't produce good fruit is cut down, and cast into the fire.

¹¹ I indeed baptize you in water for repentance, but he who comes after me is mightier than I, whose shoes I am not worthy to carry. He will baptize you in the Holy Spirit.

¹² His winnowing fork is in his hand, and he will thoroughly cleanse his threshing floor. He will gather his wheat into the barn, but the chaff he will burn up with unquenchable fire."

The Baptism of Jesus

¹³ Then Jesus came from Galilee to the Jordan to John, to be baptized by him.

¹⁴ But John would have hindered him, saying, "I need to be baptized by you, and you come to me?"

¹⁵ But Jesus, answering, said to him, "Allow it now, for this is the fitting way for us to fulfill all righteousness." Then he allowed him.

¹⁶ Jesus, when he was baptized, went up directly from the water: and behold, the heavens were opened to him. He saw the Spirit of God descending as a dove, and coming on him.

¹⁷ Behold, a voice out of the heavens said, "This is my beloved Son, with whom I am well pleased."

Who Is Jesus?

John the Baptist started to preach about six months before Jesus did. His message of repentance drew people's attention to God and prepared them for God's Son, the King of the kingdom of heaven.

The time was ripe for Jesus' coming. Many people listened to John's message and confessed their sins. The Jews used baptism as a way to initiate Gentiles into the Jewish faith, but John was also baptizing Jews who repented. His message was that they needed to repent and be baptized just as much as the Gentiles did.

John knew his calling was to prepare people for Jesus' coming. He told the crowds about Jesus' power to cleanse people from sin. Because of this, he was surprised when Jesus came to him and asked to be baptized. However, he submitted to Jesus' request.

God showed His approval by immediately sending His Spirit upon Jesus in the form of a dove. He also audibly acknowledged Jesus as His Son by speaking from heaven.

This was the beginning of Jesus' ministry on earth.

To Think About

1. What did people do when they came to John to be baptized?

2. John seemed to have some doubts that the Pharisees and Sadducees were coming to his baptisms for the right reasons. What did he tell them to do?

3. John didn't think he was worthy to baptize Jesus. Do you think Jesus was a sinner and needed to be baptized? Or did He ask for baptism to show people publicly that He was following God's plan for Him?

4. Why do you think God publicly announced at the beginning of Jesus' ministry that Jesus was His Son?

Thank you Father, for the humble example of Jesus.

JESUS IS…
a King who humbled Himself.

DAY 4

Who Is Jesus?

For in that He Himself [Jesus] has suffered,
being tempted, He is able to aid those who are
tempted. Hebrews 2:18, NKJV

READ MATTHEW 4

The Temptation of Jesus

¹ Then Jesus was led up by the Spirit into the wilderness to be tempted by the devil.

² When he had fasted forty days and forty nights, he was hungry afterward.

³ The tempter came and said to him, "If you are the Son of God, command that these stones become bread."

⁴ But he answered, "It is written, 'Man shall not live by bread alone, but by every word that proceeds out of the mouth of God.' "

⁵ Then the devil took him into the holy city. He set him on the pinnacle of the temple,

⁶ and said to him, "If you are the Son of God, throw yourself down, for it is written,

'He will command his angels concerning you.' and, 'On their hands they will bear you up, so that you don't dash your foot against a stone.' "

[7] Jesus said to him, "Again, it is written, 'You shall not test the Lord, your God.' "

[8] Again, the devil took him to an exceedingly high mountain, and showed him all the kingdoms of the world, and their glory.

[9] He said to him, "I will give you all of these things, if you will fall down and worship me."

[10] Then Jesus said to him, "Get behind me, Satan! For it is written, 'You shall worship the Lord your God, and you shall serve him only.' "

[11] Then the devil left him, and behold, angels came and served him.

Jesus Begins His Ministry

[12] Now when Jesus heard that John was delivered up, he withdrew into Galilee.

[13] Leaving Nazareth, he came and lived in Capernaum, which is by the sea, in the region of Zebulun and Naphtali,

[14] that it might be fulfilled which was spoken through Isaiah the prophet, saying,

[15] "The land of Zebulun and the land of Naphtali, toward the sea, beyond the Jordan, Galilee of the Gentiles,

[16] the people who sat in darkness saw a great light, to those who sat in the region and shadow of death, to them light has dawned."

[17] From that time, Jesus began to preach, and to say, "Repent! For the Kingdom of Heaven is at hand."

Jesus Calls the First Disciples

[18] Walking by the sea of Galilee, he saw two brothers: Simon, who is called Peter, and Andrew, his brother, casting a net into the sea; for they were fishermen.

[19] He said to them, "Come after me, and I will make you fishers for men."

[20] They immediately left their nets and followed him.

[21] Going on from there, he saw two other brothers, James the son of Zebedee, and John his brother, in the boat with Zebedee their father, mending their nets. He called them.

[22] They immediately left the boat and their father, and followed him.

Jesus Ministers to Great Crowds

[23] Jesus went about in all Galilee, teaching in their synagogues, preaching the Good

News of the Kingdom, and healing every disease and every sickness among the people.

²⁴ The report about him went out into all Syria. They brought to him all who were sick, afflicted with various diseases and torments, possessed with demons, epileptics, and paralytics; and he healed them.

²⁵ Great multitudes from Galilee, Decapolis, Jerusalem, Judea and from beyond the Jordan followed him.

Who Is Jesus?

We all know what it means to be tempted. Temptations are designed to touch us in our weakest places. In this account, the devil met Jesus in the wilderness to test Him. He tried to goad Jesus into sinning by questioning that He was the Son of God. He began each temptation by saying, "If you are the Son of God." He pointed the temptations at what he considered Jesus' greatest weaknesses.

For instance, after fasting for forty days, Jesus was hungry. So the devil aimed the first temptation at this. Then he offered Jesus a way to become famous overnight. Lastly, he offered a way for Him to rule the earth.

But Jesus answered every temptation by quoting from the Bible. Never did He follow the devil's suggestions.

In the latter part of this chapter, we see Jesus starting to call His disciples. They would spend the next few years traveling with Him and learning from Him. When He returned to heaven, they would become His apostles and be responsible for establishing His church.

Jesus called these men to leave their businesses behind and to become apprentices in the kingdom of heaven.

Jesus was a Master Teacher, but no doubt many of the people who flocked to Him were drawn by His power to heal the sick. No one had ever seen anyone do what Jesus did. He was able to heal people afflicted with all kinds of diseases and torments, as well as those who were demon-possessed.

To Think About

1. Is it ever right to follow the devil's suggestions? Why, or why not?

2. The Bible says that Jesus was tempted just as we are but didn't yield. He never sinned. What can we learn from Jesus' example that will help us overcome temptations?

3. God led Jesus to the wilderness by His Spirit. Can you think of any reasons God would have allowed His Son to be tempted like this?

4. Why might the idea of becoming "fishers of men" interest the four men whom Jesus called to follow Him in this passage? What does this tell you about Jesus?

5. Most likely more people came to Jesus for healing than to hear His teaching. Why do you think Jesus kept on healing them?

Thank you, Father, for sending a King and Savior who understands what it is like to be tempted.

JESUS IS . . . a King who was tempted as we are.

DAY 5

Who Is Jesus?

There shall come forth a Rod from the stem of Jesse, and a Branch shall grow out of His roots. The Spirit of the LORD shall rest upon Him. Isaiah 11:1–2, NKJV

READ MATTHEW 5

The Sermon on the Mount

¹ Seeing the multitudes, he went up onto the mountain. When he had sat down, his disciples came to him.

The Beatitudes

² He opened his mouth and taught them, saying,

³ "Blessed are the poor in spirit, for theirs is the Kingdom of Heaven.

⁴ Blessed are those who mourn, for they shall be comforted.

⁵ Blessed are the gentle, for they shall inherit the earth.

⁶ Blessed are those who hunger and thirst after righteousness, for they shall be filled.

[7] Blessed are the merciful, for they shall obtain mercy.

[8] Blessed are the pure in heart, for they shall see God.

[9] Blessed are the peacemakers, for they shall be called children of God.

[10] Blessed are those who have been persecuted for righteousness' sake, for theirs is the Kingdom of Heaven.

[11] "Blessed are you when people reproach you, persecute you, and say all kinds of evil against you falsely, for my sake.

[12] Rejoice, and be exceedingly glad, for great is your reward in heaven. For that is how they persecuted the prophets who were before you.

Salt and Light

[13] "You are the salt of the earth, but if the salt has lost its flavor, with what will it be salted? It is then good for nothing, but to be cast out and trodden under the feet of men.

[14] You are the light of the world. A city located on a hill can't be hidden.

[15] Neither do you light a lamp, and put it under a measuring basket, but on a stand; and it shines to all who are in the house.

[16] Even so, let your light shine before men; that they may see your good works, and glorify your Father who is in heaven.

Christ Came to Fulfill the Law

[17] "Don't think that I came to destroy the law or the prophets. I didn't come to destroy, but to fulfill.

[18] For most certainly, I tell you, until heaven and earth pass away, not even one smallest letter or one tiny pen stroke shall in any way pass away from the law, until all things are accomplished.

[19] Whoever, therefore, shall break one of these least commandments, and teach others to do so, shall be called least in the Kingdom of Heaven; but whoever shall do and teach them shall be called great in the Kingdom of Heaven.

[20] For I tell you that unless your righteousness exceeds that of the scribes and Pharisees, there is no way you will enter into the Kingdom of Heaven.

Anger

[21] "You have heard that it was said to the ancient ones, 'You shall not murder;'

and 'Whoever murders will be in danger of the judgment.'

²² But I tell you, that everyone who is angry with his brother without a cause will be in danger of the judgment; and whoever says to his brother, 'Raca!' will be in danger of the council; and whoever says, 'You fool!' will be in danger of the fire of Gehenna.

²³ "If therefore you are offering your gift at the altar, and there remember that your brother has anything against you,

²⁴ leave your gift there before the altar, and go your way. First be reconciled to your brother, and then come and offer your gift.

²⁵ Agree with your adversary quickly, while you are with him on the way; lest perhaps the prosecutor deliver you to the judge, and the judge deliver you to the officer, and you be cast into prison.

²⁶ Most certainly I tell you, you shall by no means get out of there, until you have paid the last penny.

Lust

²⁷ "You have heard that it was said, 'You shall not commit adultery;'

²⁸ but I tell you that everyone who gazes at a woman to lust after her has committed adultery with her already in his heart.

²⁹ If your right eye causes you to stumble, pluck it out and throw it away from you. For it is more profitable for you that one of your members should perish, than for your whole body to be cast into Gehenna.

³⁰ If your right hand causes you to stumble, cut it off, and throw it away from you. For it is more profitable for you that one of your members should perish, than for your whole body to be cast into Gehenna.

Divorce

³¹ "It was also said, 'Whoever shall put away his wife, let him give her a writing of divorce,'

³² but I tell you that whoever puts away his wife, except for the cause of sexual immorality, makes her an adulteress; and whoever marries her when she is put away commits adultery.

Oaths

[33] "Again you have heard that it was said to the ancient ones, 'You shall not make false vows, but shall perform to the Lord your vows,'

[34] but I tell you, don't swear at all: neither by heaven, for it is the throne of God;

[35] nor by the earth, for it is the footstool of his feet; nor by Jerusalem, for it is the city of the great King.

[36] Neither shall you swear by your head, for you can't make one hair white or black.

[37] But let your 'Yes' be 'Yes' and your 'No' be 'No.' Whatever is more than these is of the evil one.

Retaliation

[38] "You have heard that it was said, 'An eye for an eye, and a tooth for a tooth.'

[39] But I tell you, don't resist him who is evil; but whoever strikes you on your right cheek, turn to him the other also.

[40] If anyone sues you to take away your coat, let him have your cloak also.

[41] Whoever compels you to go one mile, go with him two.

[42] Give to him who asks you, and don't turn away him who desires to borrow from you.

Love Your Enemies

[43] "You have heard that it was said, 'You shall love your neighbor and hate your enemy.'

[44] But I tell you, love your enemies, bless those who curse you, do good to those who hate you, and pray for those who mistreat you and persecute you,

[45] that you may be children of your Father who is in heaven. For he makes his sun to rise on the evil and the good, and sends rain on the just and the unjust.

[46] For if you love those who love you, what reward do you have? Don't even the tax collectors do the same?

[47] If you only greet your friends, what more do you do than others? Don't even the tax collectors do the same?

[48] Therefore you shall be perfect, just as your Father in heaven is perfect.

Who Is Jesus?

This passage is the first chapter of the Sermon on the Mount.

This sermon is a summary of Jesus' teachings. It was also His way of telling them that God expected better things of His people in the kingdom of heaven than He had up until now.

Jesus is the King of the kingdom of heaven, and the Sermon on the Mount was His constitution. But before He got into the details, He described the qualities He wanted to see in the people who became part of His kingdom. He also told them what the blessings would be of becoming this kind of person (see vv. 3-12).

The standards that Jesus described in this chapter are not easy for humans to live up to. Because of this, many people don't even try. They persuade themselves that Jesus didn't really mean what He said.

God has always placed His goals beyond what people can do in their own strength. Jesus did the same in the Sermon on the Mount. This helps us realize that we need Him and His help to live up to His expectations.

Most of the teachings in this chapter are built on Old Testament laws, but Jesus gives them a spiritual dimension. For example, one Old Testament law said, "You shall not commit adultery." But Jesus said, "Don't even look at a woman to lust after her." In Jesus' kingdom, a wrong desire is as bad as a wrong action.

To Think About

This passage shows Jesus as the Master Teacher. He used figures of speech and other literary methods in his teaching to help people understand His concepts.

1. In what way should we be the salt of the earth? What sometimes happens to salt? How could this happen to us?

2. Explain how we can be lights in this world. Is our light worth anything if no one sees it?

3. Jesus goes on to talk about anger, lust, divorce, swearing of oaths, revenge, and loving our enemies. His teaching on these things is completely opposite from our natural responses. What will it do to us, and those who know us, if we obey the teachings of Jesus?

4. What kind of person would require such a standard from His followers? What does this tell us about Jesus?

5. Living for God has never been easy. But why do you think Jesus made His expectations even higher than the Old Testament did?

Thank you, Father, that we can do your will with your help, even if it seems humanly impossible.

JESUS IS…
a King who expects obedience but is willing to help us do what He asks.

DAY 6

Who Is Jesus?

He shall not judge by the sight of His eyes, nor decide
by the hearing of His ears; But with righteousness He
shall judge the poor. Isaiah 11:3–4, NKJV

READ MATTHEW 6

Giving to the Needy

[1] "Be careful that you don't do your charitable giving before men, to be seen by them, or else you have no reward from your Father who is in heaven.

[2] Therefore when you do merciful deeds, don't sound a trumpet before yourself, as the hypocrites do in the synagogues and in the streets, that they may get glory from men. Most certainly I tell you, they have received their reward.

[3] But when you do merciful deeds, don't let your left hand know what your right hand does,

[4] so that your merciful deeds may be in secret, then your Father who sees in secret will reward you openly.

The Lord's Prayer

5 "When you pray, you shall not be as the hypocrites, for they love to stand and pray in the synagogues and in the corners of the streets, that they may be seen by men. Most certainly, I tell you, they have received their reward.

6 But you, when you pray, enter into your inner room, and having shut your door, pray to your Father who is in secret, and your Father who sees in secret will reward you openly.

7 In praying, don't use vain repetitions, as the Gentiles do; for they think that they will be heard for their much speaking.

8 Therefore don't be like them, for your Father knows what things you need, before you ask him.

9 Pray like this: 'Our Father in heaven, may your name be kept holy.

10 Let your Kingdom come. Let your will be done, as in heaven, so on earth.

11 Give us today our daily bread.

12 Forgive us our debts, as we also forgive our debtors.

13 Bring us not into temptation, but deliver us from the evil one. For yours is the Kingdom, the power, and the glory forever. Amen.'

14 "For if you forgive men their trespasses, your heavenly Father will also forgive you.

15 But if you don't forgive men their trespasses, neither will your Father forgive your trespasses.

Fasting

16 "Moreover when you fast, don't be like the hypocrites, with sad faces. For they disfigure their faces, that they may be seen by men to be fasting. Most certainly I tell you, they have received their reward.

17 But you, when you fast, anoint your head, and wash your face;

18 so that you are not seen by men to be fasting, but by your Father who is in secret, and your Father, who sees in secret, will reward you.

Lay Up Treasures in Heaven

19 "Don't lay up treasures for yourselves on the earth, where moth and rust consume, and where thieves break through and steal;

²⁰ but lay up for yourselves treasures in heaven, where neither moth nor rust consume, and where thieves don't break through and steal;

²¹ for where your treasure is, there your heart will be also.

²² "The lamp of the body is the eye. If therefore your eye is sound, your whole body will be full of light.

²³ But if your eye is evil, your whole body will be full of darkness. If therefore the light that is in you is darkness, how great is the darkness!

²⁴ "No one can serve two masters, for either he will hate the one and love the other; or else he will be devoted to one and despise the other. You can't serve both God and Mammon.

Do Not Be Anxious

²⁵ Therefore I tell you, don't be anxious for your life: what you will eat, or what you will drink; nor yet for your body, what you will wear. Isn't life more than food, and the body more than clothing?

²⁶ See the birds of the sky, that they don't sow, neither do they reap, nor gather into barns. Your heavenly Father feeds them. Aren't you of much more value than they?

²⁷ "Which of you, by being anxious, can add one moment to his lifespan?

²⁸ Why are you anxious about clothing? Consider the lilies of the field, how they grow. They don't toil, neither do they spin,

²⁹ yet I tell you that even Solomon in all his glory was not dressed like one of these.

³⁰ But if God so clothes the grass of the field, which today exists, and tomorrow is thrown into the oven, won't he much more clothe you, you of little faith?

³¹ "Therefore don't be anxious, saying, 'What will we eat?', 'What will we drink?' or, 'With what will we be clothed?'

³² For the Gentiles seek after all these things; for your heavenly Father knows that you need all these things.

³³ But seek first God's Kingdom, and his righteousness; and all these things will be given to you as well.

³⁴ Therefore don't be anxious for tomorrow, for tomorrow will be anxious for

itself. Each day's own evil is sufficient.

Who Is Jesus?

This chapter of Matthew speaks about the attitudes Jesus expects in His followers. The kingdom is not made for people who try to show off their goodness. Nor does it have room for hypocrites who do good deeds and pray long prayers to impress others. Even fasting can be done for wrong reasons. Jesus wants us to do good deeds, but to do them in secret as much as possible.

Jesus had no use for selfishness either. He tells us that instead of accumulating a lot of money and possessions, we should lay up treasures in heaven. Jesus pictured money [mammon] as a slave driver. We can't serve God and money at the same time. Instead, we need to choose who will rule our lives.

Worry, or anxiety, can also rule our lives, turning us away from God. Jesus told His disciples that God looks after the birds and the flowers. Surely if He looks after them, He will also look after us.

So don't worry. Don't hoard. Don't be selfish. Let God direct your thoughts and your actions, and you will be able to sleep at night without being afraid of tomorrow.

Seek the kingdom of God and live for the King. No other life-style can satisfy like this one.

To Think About

The teachings of this chapter are not based on Old Testament laws, but are new ones that Jesus taught. But like those in chapter five, these teachings go directly against our natural way of thinking.

1. In what ways are these ideals different from the ideals of the world around us?

2. How are showing off our good deeds, being selfish, being a hypocrite, and worrying about ourselves similar to each other?[a]

3. Is following Jesus' teachings a practical way to live? Why or why not?

4. Think back over the last few days or weeks. What are some things you should have done differently according to these teachings?

Thank you, Father, for showing us how to live above selfishness, and above the fear and anxiety that is so common in the world.

JESUS IS ... a King who wants us to trust Him so He can transform us into becoming more like Him.

---

[a] They all focus on self, rather than others.

DAY 7

Who Is Jesus?

And in that day there shall be a Root of Jesse, who shall stand as a banner to the people; for the Gentiles shall seek Him, and His resting place shall be glorious. Isaiah 11:10, NKJV

READ MATTHEW 7

Judging Others

¹ "Don't judge, so that you won't be judged.

² For with whatever judgment you judge, you will be judged; and with whatever measure you measure, it will be measured to you.

³ Why do you see the speck that is in your brother's eye, but don't consider the beam that is in your own eye?

⁴ Or how will you tell your brother, 'Let me remove the speck from your eye;' and behold, the beam is in your own eye?

⁵ You hypocrite! First remove the beam out of your own eye, and then you can

see clearly to remove the speck out of your brother's eye.

[6] "Don't give that which is holy to the dogs, neither throw your pearls before the pigs, lest perhaps they trample them under their feet, and turn and tear you to pieces.

Ask, and It Will Be Given

[7] "Ask, and it will be given you. Seek, and you will find. Knock, and it will be opened for you.

[8] For everyone who asks receives. He who seeks finds. To him who knocks it will be opened.

[9] Or who is there among you, who, if his son asks him for bread, will give him a stone?

[10] Or if he asks for a fish, who will give him a serpent?

[11] If you then, being evil, know how to give good gifts to your children, how much more will your Father who is in heaven give good things to those who ask him!

The Golden Rule

[12] Therefore whatever you desire for men to do to you, you shall also do to them; for this is the law and the prophets.

[13] "Enter in by the narrow gate; for wide is the gate and broad is the way that leads to destruction, and many are those who enter in by it.

[14] How narrow is the gate, and restricted is the way that leads to life! Few are those who find it.

A Tree and Its Fruit

[15] "Beware of false prophets, who come to you in sheep's clothing, but inwardly are ravening wolves.

[16] By their fruits you will know them. Do you gather grapes from thorns, or figs from thistles?

[17] Even so, every good tree produces good fruit; but the corrupt tree produces evil fruit.

[18] A good tree can't produce evil fruit, neither can a corrupt tree produce good fruit.

[19] Every tree that doesn't grow good fruit is cut down, and thrown into the fire.

[20] Therefore by their fruits you will know them.

I Never Knew You

21 Not everyone who says to me, 'Lord, Lord,' will enter into the Kingdom of Heaven; but he who does the will of my Father who is in heaven.

22 Many will tell me in that day, 'Lord, Lord, didn't we prophesy in your name, in your name cast out demons, and in your name do many mighty works?'

23 Then I will tell them, 'I never knew you. Depart from me, you who work iniquity.'

Build Your House on the Rock

24 "Everyone therefore who hears these words of mine, and does them, I will liken him to a wise man, who built his house on a rock.

25 The rain came down, the floods came, and the winds blew, and beat on that house; and it didn't fall, for it was founded on the rock.

26 Everyone who hears these words of mine, and doesn't do them will be like a foolish man, who built his house on the sand.

27 The rain came down, the floods came, and the winds blew, and beat on that house; and it fell—and great was its fall."

The Authority of Jesus

28 When Jesus had finished saying these things, the multitudes were astonished at his teaching,

29 for he taught them with authority, and not like the scribes.

Who Is Jesus?

Jesus understands people and their inclinations. This chapter begins with people who are very critical of other people and their failures. But they don't realize, or don't care, that they have the same (or worse) problems themselves. Jesus wants us to understand how serious this is. He even used some hyperbole to get the message across. Imagine a person with a board in his eye trying to help someone else get a little piece of dirt out of his eye.

Jesus tells us to trust God and believe that He cares about us and our needs. He also wants us to care about others, just as we want them to care about us. This isn't easy to do. Most people take the easy (broad) road, but Jesus wants us to take the other road—the narrow one.

Jesus knew that some of those listening to Him would only pretend to follow Him. Jesus seems to have hated hypocrisy more than almost any other sin and warned against it many times. We can often recognize a hypocrite or a false teacher by watching how a person lives. Some people are good at pretending to serve God. They might even do miracles or preach flowery sermons. But God sees the heart and no one will fool Him.

The most important thing is that we follow Jesus' teachings ourselves. His story of the wise man and the foolish man shows very clearly that only people who genuinely serve Him can be citizens of His kingdom.

To Think About

Jesus gave these last three chapters in one setting. You might want to go back and reread all three chapters together. It will give you a better idea of what Jesus was asking His followers to be like. Remember, these were people just like you and me.

1. Jesus used many natural illustrations to help people understand His teachings. List the illustrations that stood out to you. Why did they impress you?

2. Followers of Jesus cannot be lazy. Is this a true statement? Why or why not?

3. Jesus said that not everyone can be part of the kingdom of heaven. Why are some people not able to enter the kingdom?

4. How can you build your life on the Rock? What does that mean?

Father, help me to be genuine. Help me to hear your teachings and follow them.

JESUS IS ...
a King who knows what we face in life.

DAY 8

Who Is Jesus?

And in that day you will say: Praise the LORD, call upon His name; declare His deeds among the peoples, make mention that His name is exalted. Isaiah 12:4, NKJV

READ MATTHEW 8

Jesus Cleanses a Leper

[1] When he came down from the mountain, great multitudes followed him.

[2] Behold, a leper came to him and worshiped him, saying, "Lord, if you want to, you can make me clean."

[3] Jesus stretched out his hand, and touched him, saying, "I want to. Be made clean." Immediately his leprosy was cleansed.

[4] Jesus said to him, "See that you tell nobody, but go, show yourself to the priest, and offer the gift that Moses commanded, as a testimony to them."

The Faith of a Centurion

⁵ When he came into Capernaum, a centurion came to him, asking him,

⁶ and saying, "Lord, my servant lies in the house paralyzed, grievously tormented."

⁷ Jesus said to him, "I will come and heal him."

⁸ The centurion answered, "Lord, I'm not worthy for you to come under my roof. Just say the word, and my servant will be healed.

⁹ For I am also a man under authority, having under myself soldiers. I tell this one, 'Go,' and he goes; and tell another, 'Come,' and he comes; and tell my servant, 'Do this,' and he does it."

¹⁰ When Jesus heard it, he marveled, and said to those who followed, "Most certainly I tell you, I haven't found so great a faith, not even in Israel.

¹¹ I tell you that many will come from the east and the west, and will sit down with Abraham, Isaac, and Jacob in the Kingdom of Heaven,

¹² but the children of the Kingdom will be thrown out into the outer darkness. There will be weeping and gnashing of teeth."

¹³ Jesus said to the centurion, "Go your way. Let it be done for you as you have believed." His servant was healed in that hour.

Jesus Heals Many

¹⁴ When Jesus came into Peter's house, he saw his wife's mother lying sick with a fever.

¹⁵ He touched her hand, and the fever left her. She got up and served him.

¹⁶ When evening came, they brought to him many possessed with demons. He cast out the spirits with a word, and healed all who were sick;

¹⁷ that it might be fulfilled which was spoken through Isaiah the prophet, saying, "He took our infirmities, and bore our diseases."

The Cost of Following Jesus

¹⁸ Now when Jesus saw great multitudes around him, he gave the order to depart to the other side.

¹⁹ A scribe came, and said to him, "Teacher, I will follow you wherever you go."

²⁰ Jesus said to him, "The foxes have holes, and the birds of the sky have nests,

but the Son of Man has nowhere to lay his head."

²¹ Another of his disciples said to him, "Lord, allow me first to go and bury my father."

²² But Jesus said to him, "Follow me, and leave the dead to bury their own dead."

Jesus Calms a Storm

²³ When he got into a boat, his disciples followed him.

²⁴ Behold, a violent storm came up on the sea, so much that the boat was covered with the waves, but he was asleep.

²⁵ They came to him, and woke him up, saying, "Save us, Lord! We are dying!"

²⁶ He said to them, "Why are you fearful, O you of little faith?" Then he got up, rebuked the wind and the sea, and there was a great calm.

²⁷ The men marveled, saying, "What kind of man is this, that even the wind and the sea obey him?"

Jesus Heals Two Men with Demons

²⁸ When he came to the other side, into the country of the Gergesenes, two people possessed by demons met him there, coming out of the tombs, exceedingly fierce, so that nobody could pass that way.

²⁹ Behold, they cried out, saying, "What do we have to do with you, Jesus, Son of God? Have you come here to torment us before the time?"

³⁰ Now there was a herd of many pigs feeding far away from them.

³¹ The demons begged him, saying, "If you cast us out, permit us to go away into the herd of pigs."

³² He said to them, "Go!" They came out, and went into the herd of pigs: and behold, the whole herd of pigs rushed down the cliff into the sea, and died in the water.

³³ Those who fed them fled, and went away into the city, and told everything, including what happened to those who were possessed with demons.

³⁴ Behold, all the city came out to meet Jesus. When they saw him, they begged that he would depart from their borders.

Who Is Jesus?

What kind of person does it take to convince a leper that He has the power to heal him? Or to persuade a Roman centurion that He could heal his servant without even seeing him?

It takes a special person to inspire this kind of confidence in people.

However, sometimes the people who should have the most faith have the least. The disciples had seen Jesus performing more miracles than anyone else, but it didn't dawn on them that even the wind and the stormy sea would obey Him.

If the miracle of calming the sea didn't fully persuade them, then the deliverance of the demon-possessed man surely should have. Demons were fierce opponents, and no one, not even the strongest men, dared to travel this route. But Jesus had no fear of men or demons, and the demons fled at His presence.

You would think that the local people would have welcomed Jesus after He had defeated the evil they had so long feared. But His power made them even more afraid.

Was it because He destroyed a herd of pigs that was very valuable to them? Or were they afraid He would see the evil they harbored in their hearts? Maybe they just weren't prepared to face someone with such power.

It is the same in our day. The power of Jesus inspires faith in the hearts of some people and stirs up fear in the hearts of others.

To Think About

1. Jesus said that the Roman centurion had more faith than any of the Jewish people did. Why do you think this impressed Jesus?

2. Some people thought they had faith, but when Jesus pointed out the cost of following Him, they probably realized how little they had. (vv. 18-22) Do you think you have faith in God?

3. How might a lack of faith keep you from following Jesus?

4. Why do you think Jesus' miracles stirred faith in some people but caused fear in others?

5. Which feeling does He stir up in your heart? Why?

Father, I pray that you would inspire faith in my heart. Take away any fear that is ruling me and give me more faith.

JESUS IS ...
a King who inspires faith in His followers.

DAY 9

Who Is Jesus?

Sing to the LORD, for He has done excellent things;
this is known in all the earth. Cry out and shout, O
inhabitant of Zion, for great is the Holy One of Israel
in your midst! Isaiah 12:5, 6, NKJV

READ MATTHEW 9

Jesus Heals a Paralytic

¹ He entered into a boat, and crossed over, and came into his own city.

² Behold, they brought to him a man who was paralyzed, lying on a bed. Jesus, seeing their faith, said to the paralytic, "Son, cheer up! Your sins are forgiven you."

³ Behold, some of the scribes said to themselves, "This man blasphemes."

⁴ Jesus, knowing their thoughts, said, "Why do you think evil in your hearts? .

⁵ For which is easier, to say, 'Your sins are forgiven;' or to say, 'Get up, and walk?'

^{6} But that you may know that the Son of Man has authority on earth to forgive sins—" (then he said to the paralytic), "Get up, and take up your mat, and go to your house."

^{7} He arose and departed to his house.

^{8} But when the multitudes saw it, they marveled and glorified God, who had given such authority to men.

Jesus Calls Matthew

^{9} As Jesus passed by from there, he saw a man called Matthew sitting at the tax collection office. He said to him, "Follow me." He got up and followed him.

^{10} As he sat in the house, behold, many tax collectors and sinners came and sat down with Jesus and his disciples.

^{11} When the Pharisees saw it, they said to his disciples, "Why does your teacher eat with tax collectors and sinners?"

^{12} When Jesus heard it, he said to them, "Those who are healthy have no need for a physician, but those who are sick do.

^{13} But you go and learn what this means: 'I desire mercy, and not sacrifice,' for I came not to call the righteous, but sinners to repentance."

A Question About Fasting

^{14} Then John's disciples came to him, saying, "Why do we and the Pharisees fast often, but your disciples don't fast?"

^{15} Jesus said to them, "Can the friends of the bridegroom mourn, as long as the bridegroom is with them? But the days will come when the bridegroom will be taken away from them, and then they will fast.

^{16} No one puts a piece of unshrunk cloth on an old garment; for the patch would tear away from the garment, and a worse hole is made.

^{17} Neither do people put new wine into old wine skins, or else the skins would burst, and the wine be spilled, and the skins ruined. No, they put new wine into fresh wine skins, and both are preserved."

A Girl Restored to Life and a Woman Healed

[18] While he told these things to them, behold, a ruler came and worshiped him, saying, "My daughter has just died, but come and lay your hand on her, and she will live."

[19] Jesus got up and followed him, as did his disciples.

[20] Behold, a woman who had an issue of blood for twelve years came behind him, and touched the fringe of his garment;

[21] for she said within herself, "If I just touch his garment, I will be made well."

[22] But Jesus, turning around and seeing her, said, "Daughter, cheer up! Your faith has made you well." And the woman was made well from that hour.

[23] When Jesus came into the ruler's house, and saw the flute players, and the crowd in noisy disorder,

[24] he said to them, "Make room, because the girl isn't dead, but sleeping." They were ridiculing him.

[25] But when the crowd was put out, he entered in, took her by the hand, and the girl arose.

[26] The report of this went out into all that land.

Jesus Heals Two Blind Men

[27] As Jesus passed by from there, two blind men followed him, calling out and saying, "Have mercy on us, son of David!"

[28] When he had come into the house, the blind men came to him. Jesus said to them, "Do you believe that I am able to do this?" They told him, "Yes, Lord."

[29] Then he touched their eyes, saying, "According to your faith be it done to you."

[30] Their eyes were opened. Jesus strictly commanded them, saying, "See that no one knows about this."

[31] But they went out and spread abroad his fame in all that land.

Jesus Heals a Man Unable to Speak

[32] As they went out, behold, a mute man who was demon possessed was

brought to him.

³³ When the demon was cast out, the mute man spoke. The multitudes marveled, saying, "Nothing like this has ever been seen in Israel!"

³⁴ But the Pharisees said, "By the prince of the demons, he casts out demons."

The Harvest Is Plentiful; the Laborers Few

³⁵ Jesus went about all the cities and the villages, teaching in their synagogues, and preaching the Good News of the Kingdom, and healing every disease and every sickness among the people.

³⁶ But when he saw the multitudes, he was moved with compassion for them, because they were harassed and scattered, like sheep without a shepherd.

³⁷ Then he said to his disciples, "The harvest indeed is plentiful, but the laborers are few.

³⁸ Pray therefore that the Lord of the harvest will send out laborers into his harvest."

Who Is Jesus?

Some interesting ideas and questions surface in this chapter. It seems that as Jesus looked into the heart of the paralytic, He could see that the man was yearning not only for physical healing but perhaps even more for forgiveness of his sins. Matthew gives only a few details here, but it is evident that the man and his friends had faith that Jesus could give him what he needed.

The scribes became very angry at the idea of Jesus forgiving the man's sins. Only God can forgive sins!

That's right. But that's the point. Jesus was God, so He could forgive sins. Jesus looked at this man's heart and realized that he was in need of forgiveness. He also healed him, of course, which proved his point to the scribes.

Soon afterward, Jesus called Matthew to follow him. Matthew was a tax collector, and the Jews of that day believed that all tax collectors were sinners. Then, to top it off, Matthew made a dinner and asked his sinner friends and fellow tax collectors to come and meet Jesus.

This was almost more than the Pharisees could handle. But it gave Jesus the opportunity to explain how God felt about the people Matthew had invited. They were sinners who needed salvation—and they knew it. The Pharisees, however, were blind to their own needs and refused to admit that they were sinners. By doing this, they cut themselves off from God's mercy.

As religious leaders, they should have understood how God felt about sinners. But they didn't understand God, so they failed to see their own needs.

To Think About

Jesus healed many people to show God's love for them. The rest of this chapter gives more illustrations of that. But the main point we're focusing on in this lesson is found in the first thirteen verses.

1. Do you think Jesus would have sent the paralyzed man home without healing him? Why or why not?

2. It seemed to trouble the scribes and Pharisees

when Jesus interacted with people they considered to be sinners. Why do think this was true?

3. Jesus sometimes used irony in His teaching. What do you think He was actually saying in verse 12?

4. Verses 35-38 help us understand Jesus better. What does this passage tell you about Jesus?

Lord, help me have a heart of compassion for other people like you had when you walked on the earth. Forgive me for the times I have condemned others instead of showing them your mercy and compassion.

JESUS IS ... a King who has compassion on those in need of deliverance.

DAY 10

Who Is Jesus?

Your eyes shall see your teachers. Your ears shall hear a word behind
you, saying, This is the way, walk in it. Isaiah 30:20–21, NKJV

READ MATTHEW 10

The Twelve Apostles

¹ He called to himself his twelve disciples, and gave them authority over unclean
spirits, to cast them out, and to heal every disease and every sickness.

² Now the names of the twelve apostles are these. The first, Simon, who is called
Peter; Andrew, his brother; James the son of Zebedee; John, his brother;

³ Philip; Bartholomew; Thomas; Matthew the tax collector; James the son of Alphaeus;
Lebbaeus, who was also called Thaddaeus;

⁴ Simon the Canaanite; and Judas Iscariot, who also betrayed him.

Jesus Sends Out the Twelve Apostles

⁵ Jesus sent these twelve out, and commanded them, saying, "Don't go among the

Gentiles, and don't enter into any city of the Samaritans.

⁶ Rather, go to the lost sheep of the house of Israel.

⁷ As you go, preach, saying, 'The Kingdom of Heaven is at hand!'

⁸ Heal the sick, cleanse the lepers, and cast out demons. Freely you received, so freely give.

⁹ Don't take any gold, silver, or brass in your money belts.

¹⁰ Take no bag for your journey, neither two coats, nor shoes, nor staff: for the laborer is worthy of his food.

¹¹ Into whatever city or village you enter, find out who in it is worthy; and stay there until you go on.

¹² As you enter into the household, greet it.

¹³ If the household is worthy, let your peace come on it, but if it isn't worthy, let your peace return to you.

¹⁴ Whoever doesn't receive you, nor hear your words, as you go out of that house or that city, shake the dust off your feet.

¹⁵ Most certainly I tell you, it will be more tolerable for the land of Sodom and Gomorrah in the day of judgment than for that city.

Persecution Will Come

¹⁶ "Behold, I send you out as sheep among wolves. Therefore be wise as serpents, and harmless as doves.

¹⁷ But beware of men: for they will deliver you up to councils, and in their synagogues they will scourge you.

¹⁸ Yes, and you will be brought before governors and kings for my sake, for a testimony to them and to the nations.

¹⁹ But when they deliver you up, don't be anxious how or what you will say, for it will be given you in that hour what you will say.

²⁰ For it is not you who speak, but the Spirit of your Father who speaks in you.

²¹ "Brother will deliver up brother to death, and the father his child. Children will rise up against parents, and cause them to be put to death.

²² You will be hated by all men for my name's sake, but he who endures to the end will be saved.

²³ But when they persecute you in this city, flee into the next, for most certainly I tell you, you will not have gone through the cities of Israel, until the Son of Man has come.

²⁴ "A disciple is not above his teacher, nor a servant above his lord.

²⁵ It is enough for the disciple that he be like his teacher, and the servant like his lord. If they have called the master of the house Beelzebul, how much more those of his household!

Have No Fear

²⁶ Therefore don't be afraid of them, for there is nothing covered that will not be revealed; and hidden that will not be known.

²⁷ What I tell you in the darkness, speak in the light; and what you hear whispered in the ear, proclaim on the housetops.

²⁸ Don't be afraid of those who kill the body, but are not able to kill the soul. Rather, fear him who is able to destroy both soul and body in Gehenna.

²⁹ "Aren't two sparrows sold for an assarion coin? Not one of them falls on the ground apart from your Father's will,

³⁰ but the very hairs of your head are all numbered.

³¹ Therefore don't be afraid. You are of more value than many sparrows.

³² Everyone therefore who confesses me before men, him I will also confess before my Father who is in heaven.

³³ But whoever denies me before men, him I will also deny before my Father who is in heaven.

Not Peace, but a Sword

³⁴ "Don't think that I came to send peace on the earth. I didn't come to send peace, but a sword.

³⁵ For I came to set a man at odds against his father, and a daughter against her mother, and a daughter-in-law against her mother-in-law.

³⁶ A man's foes will be those of his own household.

³⁷ He who loves father or mother more than me is not worthy of me; and he who loves son or daughter more than me isn't worthy of me.

³⁸ He who doesn't take his cross and follow after me, isn't worthy of me.

³⁹ He who seeks his life will lose it; and he who loses his life for my sake will find it.

Rewards

⁴⁰ He who receives you receives me, and he who receives me receives him who sent me.

⁴¹ He who receives a prophet in the name of a prophet will receive a prophet's reward. He who receives a righteous man in the name of a righteous man will receive a righteous man's reward.

⁴² Whoever gives one of these little ones just a cup of cold water to drink in the name of a disciple, most certainly I tell you he will in no way lose his reward."

Who Is Jesus?

Jesus' disciples were in training. Jesus was probably about half-way through His ministry by now, and it was time for them to start putting into practice what they had learned from Him.

This chapter records the final instructions Jesus gave His disciples before He sent them out to tell others about the kingdom of heaven. He wanted them to understand that He wasn't sending them on a vacation. This mission was serious, and any expectation they had of novelty or glamor would soon wear off.

Jesus told them they would face opposition. Ten of these twelve men would later die a martyr's death because of the ministry He was giving them. They would be hated, they would be beaten, they would be betrayed by their family and friends, and they would be driven from city to city. But Jesus promised to be with them in spirit and give them words to speak. He also gave them power to perform miracles.

In contrast to our day, the disciples were not supported by some large, rich church. Jesus told them to go without money, without food, and without extra clothing or shoes. He promised them none of the securities that missionaries receive today.

They were on their own. They had no one but God to depend on.

Was He asking too much of them? No, because He didn't ask more of them than He asked of Himself. He too owned nothing except the clothing on His back. He too was ridiculed and persecuted. He too was going to die.

To Think About

1. How were Jesus' instructions to the disciples different from those given to most modern missionaries?

2. The disciples were sent out as sheep in the midst of wolves. In what ways was this an accurate figure of speech? How were they to cope with this?

3. Who were they to fear? Who were they not to fear? Why?

4. What are some wrong reasons for people being missionaries?

Help me, Lord, to be willing to be persecuted and killed for your sake. Help me to carry my cross even as you did, in love and without fear.

JESUS IS ... a King who knows what it means to be hated, persecuted, and killed.

DAY 11

Who Is Jesus?

Strengthen the weak hands, and make firm the feeble knees. Say to those who are fearful-hearted, Be strong, do not fear! Isaiah 35:3-4, NKJV

READ MATTHEW 11

Messengers from John the Baptist

¹ When Jesus had finished directing his twelve disciples, he departed from there to teach and preach in their cities.

² Now when John heard in the prison the works of Christ, he sent two of his disciples

³ and said to him, "Are you he who comes, or should we look for another?"

⁴ Jesus answered them, "Go and tell John the things which you hear and see:

⁵ the blind receive their sight, the lame walk, the lepers are cleansed, the deaf hear, the dead are raised up, and the poor have good news preached to them.

⁶ Blessed is he who finds no occasion for stumbling in me."

⁷ As these went their way, Jesus began to say to the multitudes concerning John, "What did you go out into the wilderness to see? A reed shaken by the wind?

⁸ But what did you go out to see? A man in soft clothing? Behold, those who wear soft clothing are in kings' houses.

⁹ But why did you go out? To see a prophet? Yes, I tell you, and much more than a prophet.

¹⁰ For this is he, of whom it is written, 'Behold, I send my messenger before your face, who will prepare your way before you.'

¹¹ Most certainly I tell you, among those who are born of women there has not arisen anyone greater than John the Baptizer; yet he who is least in the Kingdom of Heaven is greater than he.

¹² From the days of John the Baptizer until now, the Kingdom of Heaven suffers violence, and the violent take it by force.

¹³ For all the prophets and the law prophesied until John.

¹⁴ If you are willing to receive it, this is Elijah, who is to come.

¹⁵ He who has ears to hear, let him hear.

¹⁶ "But to what shall I compare this generation? It is like children sitting in the marketplaces, who call to their companions

¹⁷ and say, 'We played the flute for you, and you didn't dance. We mourned for you, and you didn't lament.'

¹⁸ For John came neither eating nor drinking, and they say, 'He has a demon.'

¹⁹ The Son of Man came eating and drinking, and they say, 'Behold, a gluttonous man and a drunkard, a friend of tax collectors and sinners!' But wisdom is justified by her children."

Woe to Unrepentant Cities

²⁰ Then he began to denounce the cities in which most of his mighty works had been done, because they didn't repent.

²¹ "Woe to you, Chorazin! Woe to you, Bethsaida! For if the mighty works

had been done in Tyre and Sidon which were done in you, they would have repented long ago in sackcloth and ashes.

²² But I tell you, it will be more tolerable for Tyre and Sidon on the day of judgment than for you.

²³ You, Capernaum, who are exalted to heaven, you will go down to Hades. For if the mighty works had been done in Sodom which were done in you, it would have remained until today.

²⁴ But I tell you that it will be more tolerable for the land of Sodom, on the day of judgment, than for you."

Come to Me, and I Will Give You Rest

²⁵ At that time, Jesus answered, "I thank you, Father, Lord of heaven and earth, that you hid these things from the wise and understanding, and revealed them to infants.

²⁶ Yes, Father, for so it was well-pleasing in your sight.

²⁷ All things have been delivered to me by my Father. No one knows the Son, except the Father; neither does anyone know the Father, except the Son, and he to whom the Son desires to reveal him.

²⁸ "Come to me, all you who labor and are heavily burdened, and I will give you rest.

²⁹ Take my yoke upon you, and learn from me, for I am gentle and humble in heart; and you will find rest for your souls.

³⁰ For my yoke is easy, and my burden is light."

Who Is Jesus?

John the Baptist was in prison and discouraged. In fact, he was beginning to wonder if he had been wrong about Jesus. Maybe someone else was coming to be the Messiah. He decided to send two of his disciples to ask Jesus.

Jesus didn't condemn John for his doubts. Instead, he

told John's disciples to watch Him for a while. Then he told them to go back to John and tell him about the miracles He was doing and the people He was helping. That way John could draw his own conclusions.

Jesus didn't flatter John, but He did talk to the multitudes about him after John's disciples left. John was the last and the greatest of the Old Testament prophets. God had a special plan for him to be the forerunner of the Messiah. But now the Messiah had come, and John's work was almost finished.

Then Jesus went on to talk about the Jewish cities He had preached in and how they would largely reject Him. He compared them to Tyre and Sidon, and also to Sodom. Those cities had been so sinful that God had destroyed them. Yet Jesus said that if those cities had seen and heard what He had done in the Jewish cities, they would have repented.

However, the door was still open, and the chapter ends with the great invitation of the Gospel. Everyone was invited. They could trade their burdens for peace and rest.

So can you.

To Think About

1. Why would Jesus not have scolded John for his doubts?

2. Do you think Jesus' answer helped John? Explain your answer.

3. Why would wicked cities like Sodom be less accountable than the Jewish cities that Jesus mentioned?

4. Despite the Jews' rejection of Jesus and their guilt, Jesus still invited them to come to Him for salvation. What does this tell you about God?

Thank you, Lord, for your understanding, your patience, and your invitation to find rest.

JESUS IS ... a King who invites everyone to find salvation by joining Him.

DAY 12

Who Is Jesus?

Then the eyes of the blind shall be opened, and the ears of the deaf shall be unstopped. Then the lame shall leap like a deer, and the tongue of the dumb sing. For waters shall burst forth in the wilderness, and streams in the desert. Isaiah 35:5–6, NKJV

READ MATTHEW 12

Jesus Is Lord of the Sabbath

¹ At that time, Jesus went on the Sabbath day through the grain fields. His disciples were hungry and began to pluck heads of grain and to eat.

² But the Pharisees, when they saw it, said to him, "Behold, your disciples do what is not lawful to do on the Sabbath."

³ But he said to them, "Haven't you read what David did, when he was hungry, and those who were with him;

⁴ how he entered into God's house, and ate the show bread, which was not lawful for him to eat, neither for those who were with him, but only for the priests?

⁵ Or have you not read in the law, that on the Sabbath day, the priests in the temple profane the Sabbath, and are guiltless?

⁶ But I tell you that one greater than the temple is here.

⁷ But if you had known what this means, 'I desire mercy, and not sacrifice,' you wouldn't have condemned the guiltless.

⁸ For the Son of Man is Lord of the Sabbath."

A Man with a Withered Hand

⁹ He departed there, and went into their synagogue.

¹⁰ And behold there was a man with a withered hand. They asked him, "Is it lawful to heal on the Sabbath day?" that they might accuse him.

¹¹ He said to them, "What man is there among you, who has one sheep, and if this one falls into a pit on the Sabbath day, won't he grab on to it, and lift it out?

¹² Of how much more value then is a man than a sheep! Therefore it is lawful to do good on the Sabbath day."

¹³ Then he told the man, "Stretch out your hand." He stretched it out; and it was restored whole, just like the other.

¹⁴ But the Pharisees went out, and conspired against him, how they might destroy him.

God's Chosen Servant

¹⁵ Jesus, perceiving that, withdrew from there. Great multitudes followed him; and he healed them all,

¹⁶ and commanded them that they should not make him known:

¹⁷ that it might be fulfilled which was spoken through Isaiah the prophet, saying,

¹⁸ "Behold, my servant whom I have chosen; my beloved in whom my soul is well pleased: I will put my Spirit on him. He will proclaim justice to the nations.

¹⁹ He will not strive, nor shout; neither will anyone hear his voice in the streets.

²⁰ He won't break a bruised reed. He won't quench a smoking flax, until he leads justice to victory.

²¹ In his name, the nations will hope."

Blasphemy Against the Holy Spirit

22 Then one possessed by a demon, blind and mute, was brought to him and he healed him, so that the blind and mute man both spoke and saw.

23 All the multitudes were amazed, and said, "Can this be the son of David?"

24 But when the Pharisees heard it, they said, "This man does not cast out demons, except by Beelzebul, the prince of the demons."

25 Knowing their thoughts, Jesus said to them, "Every kingdom divided against itself is brought to desolation, and every city or house divided against itself will not stand.

26 If Satan casts out Satan, he is divided against himself. How then will his kingdom stand?

27 If I by Beelzebul cast out demons, by whom do your children cast them out? Therefore they will be your judges.

28 But if I by the Spirit of God cast out demons, then God's Kingdom has come upon you.

29 Or how can one enter into the house of the strong man, and plunder his goods, unless he first bind the strong man? Then he will plunder his house.

30 "He who is not with me is against me, and he who doesn't gather with me, scatters.

31 Therefore I tell you, every sin and blasphemy will be forgiven men, but the blasphemy against the Spirit will not be forgiven men.

32 Whoever speaks a word against the Son of Man, it will be forgiven him; but whoever speaks against the Holy Spirit, it will not be forgiven him, neither in this age, nor in that which is to come.

A Tree Is Known by Its Fruit

33 "Either make the tree good, and its fruit good, or make the tree corrupt, and its fruit corrupt; for the tree is known by its fruit.

34 You offspring of vipers, how can you, being evil, speak good things? For out of the abundance of the heart, the mouth speaks.

35 The good man out of his good treasure brings out good things, and the evil

man out of his evil treasure brings out evil things.

³⁶ I tell you that every idle word that men speak, they will give account of it in the day of judgment.

³⁷ For by your words you will be justified, and by your words you will be condemned."

The Sign of Jonah

³⁸ Then certain of the scribes and Pharisees answered, "Teacher, we want to see a sign from you."

³⁹ But he answered them, "An evil and adulterous generation seeks after a sign, but no sign will be given to it but the sign of Jonah the prophet.

⁴⁰ For as Jonah was three days and three nights in the belly of the whale, so will the Son of Man be three days and three nights in the heart of the earth.

⁴¹ The men of Nineveh will stand up in the judgment with this generation, and will condemn it, for they repented at the preaching of Jonah; and behold, someone greater than Jonah is here.

⁴² The queen of the south will rise up in the judgment with this generation, and will condemn it, for she came from the ends of the earth to hear the wisdom of Solomon; and behold, someone greater than Solomon is here.

Return of an Unclean Spirit

⁴³ When an unclean spirit has gone out of a man, he passes through waterless places, seeking rest, and doesn't find it.

⁴⁴ Then he says, 'I will return into my house from which I came out,' and when he has come back, he finds it empty, swept, and put in order.

⁴⁵ Then he goes, and takes with himself seven other spirits more evil than he is, and they enter in and dwell there. The last state of that man becomes worse than the first. Even so will it be also to this evil generation."

Jesus' Mother and Brothers

⁴⁶ While he was yet speaking to the multitudes, behold, his mother and his brothers stood outside, seeking to speak to him.

⁴⁷ One said to him, "Behold, your mother and your brothers stand outside,

seeking to speak to you."

⁴⁸ But he answered him who spoke to him, "Who is my mother? Who are my brothers?"

⁴⁹ He stretched out his hand towards his disciples, and said, "Behold, my mother and my brothers!

⁵⁰ For whoever does the will of my Father who is in heaven, he is my brother, and sister, and mother."

Who Is Jesus?

In this reading we see the disagreements between Jesus and the Pharisees beginning to intensify. This chapter records four clashes between them. The first two concerned the Sabbath day, while the next one dealt with the question of where Jesus got His power. The last one occurred when the Pharisees asked Jesus for a sign that His power came from God.

The Pharisees had put together a very detailed list of rules that they required people to obey. Many of the confrontations Jesus had with them had to do with these rules. He believed that showing mercy and meeting people's needs were more important than unreasonable rules and regulations.

The Pharisees then accused Jesus of getting His power from the devil and started to discuss ways of getting rid of Him.

Jesus hated hypocrisy. He knew that the Pharisees treated their animals better than they treated fellow human beings. Did God forbid people to do good on the Sabbath? Did He mean for people to go hungry rather than break the Sabbath laws? Was it wrong to heal a sick person on the Sabbath? Jesus knew that these things were not God's plan.

To Think About

1. The Pharisees looked after the needs of their animals on the Sabbath day, but condemned Jesus for helping people on the Sabbath day. How did this show their inconsistency?

2. Why do you think it was inconsistent of the Pharisees to accuse Jesus of getting His power from Beelzebub (the devil)?

3. Why is it dangerous to attribute God's work to the devil? Is it also dangerous to attribute the devil's work to God? Can you think of any ways we might do this today?

Help me, Lord, to renounce any hypocrisy in my life and to serve you rather than self. Help me to be merciful.

JESUS IS ... a King who has mercy on the needy.

DAY 13

Who Is Jesus?

And He said, "Go, and tell this people: 'Keep on hearing, but do not understand; keep on seeing, but do not perceive.' Make the heart of this people dull, and their ears heavy, and shut their eyes; lest they see with their eyes, and hear with their ears, and understand with their heart, and return and be healed." Isaiah 6:9–10, NKJV

Introduction

A parable is "a simple story used to illustrate a moral or spiritual lesson." This chapter includes a number of parables that Jesus used to explain truth to people who wanted to understand.

The disciples wondered why He used these stories, so He explained the first one to them. He also explained why He used this teaching method.

Jesus wasn't interested in just entertaining the crowd. He wanted them to think about what He was saying. The stories were simple enough that people who wanted to know the truth could figure them out. The stories also helped people to remember what He taught them.

Each of these parables teaches an important truth about life. Read them carefully so you don't miss what Jesus is saying to you.

READ MATTHEW 13

The Parable of the Sower

¹ On that day Jesus went out of the house, and sat by the seaside.

² Great multitudes gathered to him, so that he entered into a boat, and sat, and all the multitude stood on the beach.

³ He spoke to them many things in parables, saying, "Behold, a farmer went out to sow.

⁴ As he sowed, some seeds fell by the roadside, and the birds came and devoured them.

⁵ Others fell on rocky ground, where they didn't have much soil, and immediately they sprang up, because they had no depth of earth.

⁶ When the sun had risen, they were scorched. Because they had no root, they withered away.

⁷ Others fell among thorns. The thorns grew up and choked them.

⁸ Others fell on good soil, and yielded fruit: some one hundred times as much, some sixty, and some thirty.

⁹ He who has ears to hear, let him hear."

The Purpose of the Parables

¹⁰ The disciples came, and said to him, "Why do you speak to them in parables?"

¹¹ He answered them, "To you it is given to know the mysteries of the Kingdom of Heaven, but it is not given to them.

¹² For whoever has, to him will be given, and he will have abundance, but whoever doesn't have, from him will be taken away even that which he has.

¹³ Therefore I speak to them in parables, because seeing they don't see, and hearing, they don't hear, neither do they understand.

[14] In them the prophecy of Isaiah is fulfilled, which says, 'By hearing you will hear, and will in no way understand; Seeing you will see, and will in no way perceive:

[15] for this people's heart has grown callous, their ears are dull of hearing, they have closed their eyes; or else perhaps they might perceive with their eyes, hear with their ears, understand with their heart, and would turn again; and I would heal them.'

[16] "But blessed are your eyes, for they see; and your ears, for they hear.

[17] For most certainly I tell you that many prophets and righteous men desired to see the things which you see, and didn't see them; and to hear the things which you hear, and didn't hear them.

The Parable of the Sower Explained

[18] "Hear, then, the parable of the farmer.

[19] When anyone hears the word of the Kingdom, and doesn't understand it, the evil one comes, and snatches away that which has been sown in his heart. This is what was sown by the roadside.

[20] What was sown on the rocky places, this is he who hears the word, and immediately with joy receives it;

[21] yet he has no root in himself, but endures for a while. When oppression or persecution arises because of the word, immediately he stumbles.

[22] What was sown among the thorns, this is he who hears the word, but the cares of this age and the deceitfulness of riches choke the word, and he becomes unfruitful.

[23] What was sown on the good ground, this is he who hears the word, and understands it, who most certainly bears fruit, and produces, some one hundred times as much, some sixty, and some thirty."

The Parable of the Weeds

[24] He set another parable before them, saying, "The Kingdom of Heaven is like a man who sowed good seed in his field,

[25] but while people slept, his enemy came and sowed darnel weeds also among the wheat, and went away.

[26] But when the blade sprang up and produced fruit, then the darnel weeds appeared also.

^{27} The servants of the householder came and said to him, 'Sir, didn't you sow good seed in your field? Where did these darnel weeds come from?'

^{28} "He said to them, 'An enemy has done this.' "The servants asked him, 'Do you want us to go and gather them up?'

^{29} "But he said, 'No, lest perhaps while you gather up the darnel weeds, you root up the wheat with them.

^{30} Let both grow together until the harvest, and in the harvest time I will tell the reapers, "First, gather up the darnel weeds, and bind them in bundles to burn them; but gather the wheat into my barn." ' "

The Mustard Seed and the Leaven

^{31} He set another parable before them, saying, "The Kingdom of Heaven is like a grain of mustard seed, which a man took, and sowed in his field;

^{32} which indeed is smaller than all seeds. But when it is grown, it is greater than the herbs, and becomes a tree, so that the birds of the air come and lodge in its branches."

^{33} He spoke another parable to them. "The Kingdom of Heaven is like yeast, which a woman took, and hid in three measures of meal, until it was all leavened."

Prophecy and Parables

^{34} Jesus spoke all these things in parables to the multitudes; and without a parable, he didn't speak to them,

^{35} that it might be fulfilled which was spoken through the prophet, saying, "I will open my mouth in parables; I will utter things hidden from the foundation of the world."

The Parable of the Weeds Explained

^{36} Then Jesus sent the multitudes away, and went into the house. His disciples came to him, saying, "Explain to us the parable of the darnel weeds of the field."

^{37} He answered them, "He who sows the good seed is the Son of Man,

^{38} the field is the world; and the good seed, these are the children of the Kingdom; and the darnel weeds are the children of the evil one.

^{39} The enemy who sowed them is the devil. The harvest is the end of the age, and the reapers are angels.

^{40} As therefore the darnel weeds are gathered up and burned with fire; so will it be at the end of this age.

[41] The Son of Man will send out his angels, and they will gather out of his Kingdom all things that cause stumbling, and those who do iniquity,

[42] and will cast them into the furnace of fire. There will be weeping and the gnashing of teeth.

[43] Then the righteous will shine like the sun in the Kingdom of their Father. He who has ears to hear, let him hear.

The Parable of the Hidden Treasure

[44] "Again, the Kingdom of Heaven is like treasure hidden in the field, which a man found, and hid. In his joy, he goes and sells all that he has, and buys that field.

The Parable of the Pearl of Great Value

[45] "Again, the Kingdom of Heaven is like a man who is a merchant seeking fine pearls,

[46] who having found one pearl of great price, he went and sold all that he had, and bought it.

The Parable of the Net

[47] "Again, the Kingdom of Heaven is like a dragnet, that was cast into the sea, and gathered some fish of every kind,

[48] which, when it was filled, they drew up on the beach. They sat down, and gathered the good into containers, but the bad they threw away.

[49] So will it be in the end of the world. The angels will come and separate the wicked from among the righteous,

[50] and will cast them into the furnace of fire. There will be the weeping and the gnashing of teeth."

New and Old Treasures

[51] Jesus said to them, "Have you understood all these things?" They answered him, "Yes, Lord."

[52] He said to them, "Therefore every scribe who has been made a disciple in the Kingdom of Heaven is like a man who is a householder, who brings out of his treasure new and old things."

Jesus Rejected at Nazareth

[53] When Jesus had finished these parables, he departed from there.

[54] Coming into his own country, he taught them in their synagogue, so that they were astonished, and said, "Where did this man get this wisdom, and these mighty works?

[55] Isn't this the carpenter's son? Isn't his mother called Mary, and his brothers, James, Joses, Simon, and Judas?

[56] Aren't all of his sisters with us? Where then did this man get all of these things?"

[57] They were offended by him. But Jesus said to them, "A prophet is not without honor, except in his own country, and in his own house."

[58] He didn't do many mighty works there because of their unbelief.

Who Is Jesus?

Jesus was a Master Teacher. This chapter shows one of his teaching methods—teaching by telling stories. As you read this chapter, you will notice that His stories were about ordinary things that people understood. For instance, the parable of the sower is about a farmer sowing a field. Probably everyone in his audience had either done this or seen it done.

The parable of the weeds was also about sowing seeds, but from a different perspective. Again, Jesus' audience should have been able to picture the story, even if they had never seen it happen.

Everyone in Israel was familiar with a mustard seed. They knew how tiny the seed was and how large the mustard tree was when it was full grown. The women in the audience would certainly have understood how leaven worked, and how a small amount would spread through a batch of dough.

Most children and many adults have dreamed of finding a hidden treasure. They can identify with the next two stories.

And finally, at least some in the crowd were probably fishermen and had seen for themselves the garbage that a net could bring in along with a catch of fish.

But that was only the surface. If they wanted a deeper understanding of the truths Jesus was telling them, they would have to take time to really think about the stories.

It is the same for us.

To Think About

Here is a list of the parables in this chapter. Write a sentence for each parable that explains the basic point Jesus was making.

1. The parable of the sower (vv. 1-9, explained in 18-23)

2. The parable of the weeds (vv. 24-30, explained in 36-43)

3. The parable of the mustard seed (vv. 31, 32)

4. The parable of the leaven (v. 33)

5. The parable of the hidden treasure (v. 44)

6. The parable of the pearl of great price (vv. 45, 46)

7. The parable of the net (vv. 47-50)

Father, give me understanding of the truths you want to teach me.

JESUS IS ... a King
who knows how to teach us
lessons that we will not forget.

DAY 14

Who Is Jesus?

Even the youths shall faint and be weary, and the young men shall utterly fall, But those who wait on the LORD shall renew their strength; they shall mount up with wings like eagles, they shall run and not be weary, they shall walk and not faint. Isaiah 40:30–31, NKJV

Introduction

Chapter thirteen focused on Jesus' teaching. This chapter focuses on His miracles.

READ MATTHEW 14

The Death of John the Baptist

¹ At that time, Herod the tetrarch heard the report concerning Jesus,

² and said to his servants, "This is John the Baptizer. He is risen from the dead. That is why these powers work in him."

³ For Herod had laid hold of John, and bound him, and put him in prison for the

sake of Herodias, his brother Philip's wife.

⁴ For John said to him, "It is not lawful for you to have her."

⁵ When he would have put him to death, he feared the multitude, because they counted him as a prophet.

⁶ But when Herod's birthday came, the daughter of Herodias danced among them and pleased Herod.

⁷ Whereupon he promised with an oath to give her whatever she should ask.

⁸ She, being prompted by her mother, said, "Give me here on a platter the head of John the Baptizer."

⁹ The king was grieved, but for the sake of his oaths, and of those who sat at the table with him, he commanded it to be given,

¹⁰ and he sent and beheaded John in the prison.

¹¹ His head was brought on a platter, and given to the young lady: and she brought it to her mother.

¹² His disciples came, and took the body, and buried it; and they went and told Jesus.

Jesus Feeds the Five Thousand

¹³ Now when Jesus heard this, he withdrew from there in a boat, to a deserted place apart. When the multitudes heard it, they followed him on foot from the cities.

¹⁴ Jesus went out, and he saw a great multitude. He had compassion on them, and healed their sick.

¹⁵ When evening had come, his disciples came to him, saying, "This place is deserted, and the hour is already late. Send the multitudes away, that they may go into the villages, and buy themselves food."

¹⁶ But Jesus said to them, "They don't need to go away. You give them something to eat."

¹⁷ They told him, "We only have here five loaves and two fish."

¹⁸ He said, "Bring them here to me."

¹⁹ He commanded the multitudes to sit down on the grass; and he took the five loaves and the two fish, and looking up to heaven, he blessed, broke and gave the loaves to the disciples, and the disciples gave to the multitudes.

²⁰ They all ate, and were filled. They took up twelve baskets full of that which

remained left over from the broken pieces.

²¹ Those who ate were about five thousand men, in addition to women and children.

Jesus Walks on the Water

²² Immediately Jesus made the disciples get into the boat, and to go ahead of him to the other side, while he sent the multitudes away.

²³ After he had sent the multitudes away, he went up into the mountain by himself to pray. When evening had come, he was there alone.

²⁴ But the boat was now in the middle of the sea, distressed by the waves, for the wind was contrary.

²⁵ In the fourth watch of the night, Jesus came to them, walking on the sea.

²⁶ When the disciples saw him walking on the sea, they were troubled, saying, "It's a ghost!" and they cried out for fear.

²⁷ But immediately Jesus spoke to them, saying, "Cheer up! It is I! Don't be afraid."

²⁸ Peter answered him and said, "Lord, if it is you, command me to come to you on the waters."

²⁹ He said, "Come!" Peter stepped down from the boat, and walked on the waters to come to Jesus.

³⁰ But when he saw that the wind was strong, he was afraid, and beginning to sink, he cried out, saying, "Lord, save me!"

³¹ Immediately Jesus stretched out his hand, took hold of him, and said to him, "You of little faith, why did you doubt?"

³² When they got up into the boat, the wind ceased.

³³ Those who were in the boat came and worshiped him, saying, "You are truly the Son of God!"

Jesus Heals the Sick in Gennesaret

³⁴ When they had crossed over, they came to the land of Gennesaret.

³⁵ When the people of that place recognized him, they sent into all that surrounding region, and brought to him all who were sick;

³⁶ and they begged him that they might just touch the fringe of his garment. As many as touched it were made whole.

Who Is Jesus?

Jesus was the Son of God, but He was also a man—so He had emotions as a man. When the news came of His friend John the Baptist's sudden death, it hit Jesus hard. He felt a need of some time alone with His closest friends, the disciples.

But it wasn't to be. People saw Him leave and guessed His destination. While He and the disciples took a boat across the water, the multitudes ran around the lake on the shore. When Jesus got to where He wanted to go, the people were there waiting for Him.

Instead of having time to relax and grieve in solitude, Jesus put His desires behind Him and ministered to the needs of the people.

This was typical. Jesus had a heart of compassion for all people—the physically ill, those who were in spiritual bondage, and those who were simply poor and needy. The needs of those who came to Him for help always took priority over His own needs.

The disciples were troubled by this and wanted to send the multitudes back to the cities for the night. But Jesus didn't want to let them go hungry.

So He fed them all—five thousand men, along with the women and children who were present—with five loaves and two fish. The Gospel of John tells us that this was the lunch of a young lad. Jesus multiplied this meager lunch so it was enough for everyone. In fact, afterwards they gathered up twelve baskets of left-over fragments.

But that wasn't the end of the miracles for that day. When

they were done eating, Jesus sent everyone away, including the disciples, who took the boat. Jesus stayed behind, probably taking this chance to get the solitude He had been longing for.

Finally, toward morning, Jesus followed the disciples. He took the short route. Straight across the lake.

To Think About

1.   Why didn't Jesus tell the multitudes to leave Him alone and go home?

2.   What can you learn from Jesus' example?

3.   Why do you think Peter started to sink all of a sudden?

Father, help me to have a heart for the needy
people around me like Jesus did.

JESUS IS ... a King who cared more for other people's needs than He did for His own.

DAY 15

Who Is Jesus?

Behold! My Servant whom I uphold, My Elect One in whom My soul delights! I have put My Spirit upon Him; He will bring forth justice to the Gentiles. Isaiah 42:1, NKJV

READ MATTHEW 15

Traditions and Commandments

¹ Then Pharisees and scribes came to Jesus from Jerusalem, saying,

² "Why do your disciples disobey the tradition of the elders? For they don't wash their hands when they eat bread."

³ He answered them, "Why do you also disobey the commandment of God because of your tradition?

⁴ For God commanded, 'Honor your father and your mother,' and, 'He who speaks evil of father or mother, let him be put to death.'

⁵ But you say, 'Whoever may tell his father or his mother, "Whatever help you

might otherwise have gotten from me is a gift devoted to God,"

[6] he shall not honor his father or mother.' You have made the commandment of God void because of your tradition.

[7] You hypocrites! Well did Isaiah prophesy of you, saying,

[8] 'These people draw near to me with their mouth, and honor me with their lips; but their heart is far from me.

[9] And in vain do they worship me, teaching as doctrine rules made by men.' "

What Defiles a Person

[10] He summoned the multitude, and said to them, "Hear, and understand.

[11] That which enters into the mouth doesn't defile the man; but that which proceeds out of the mouth, this defiles the man."

[12] Then the disciples came, and said to him, "Do you know that the Pharisees were offended, when they heard this saying?"

[13] But he answered, "Every plant which my heavenly Father didn't plant will be uprooted.

[14] Leave them alone. They are blind guides of the blind. If the blind guide the blind, both will fall into a pit."

[15] Peter answered him, "Explain the parable to us."

[16] So Jesus said, "Do you also still not understand?

[17] Don't you understand that whatever goes into the mouth passes into the belly, and then out of the body?

[18] But the things which proceed out of the mouth come out of the heart, and they defile the man.

[19] For out of the heart come evil thoughts, murders, adulteries, sexual sins, thefts, false testimony, and blasphemies.

[20] These are the things which defile the man; but to eat with unwashed hands doesn't defile the man."

The Faith of a Canaanite Woman

[21] Jesus went out from there, and withdrew into the region of Tyre and Sidon.

[22] Behold, a Canaanite woman came out from those borders, and cried, saying,

"Have mercy on me, Lord, you son of David! My daughter is severely possessed by a demon!"

23 But he answered her not a word. His disciples came and begged him, saying, "Send her away; for she cries after us."

24 But he answered, "I wasn't sent to anyone but the lost sheep of the house of Israel."

25 But she came and worshiped him, saying, "Lord, help me."

26 But he answered, "It is not appropriate to take the children's bread and throw it to the dogs."

27 But she said, "Yes, Lord, but even the dogs eat the crumbs which fall from their masters' table."

28 Then Jesus answered her, "Woman, great is your faith! Be it done to you even as you desire." And her daughter was healed from that hour.

Jesus Heals Many

29 Jesus departed from there, and came near to the sea of Galilee; and he went up into the mountain, and sat there.

30 Great multitudes came to him, having with them the lame, blind, mute, maimed, and many others, and they put them down at his feet. He healed them,

31 so that the multitude wondered when they saw the mute speaking, the injured healed, the lame walking, and the blind seeing—and they glorified the God of Israel.

Jesus Feeds the Four Thousand

32 Jesus summoned his disciples and said, "I have compassion on the multitude, because they continue with me now three days and have nothing to eat. I don't want to send them away fasting, or they might faint on the way."

33 The disciples said to him, "Where should we get so many loaves in a deserted place as to satisfy so great a multitude?"

34 Jesus said to them, "How many loaves do you have?" They said, "Seven, and a few small fish."

35 He commanded the multitude to sit down on the ground;

36 and he took the seven loaves and the fish. He gave thanks and broke them,

and gave to the disciples, and the disciples to the multitudes.

³⁷ They all ate, and were filled. They took up seven baskets full of the broken pieces that were left over.

³⁸ Those who ate were four thousand men, in addition to women and children.

³⁹ Then he sent away the multitudes, got into the boat, and came into the borders of Magdala.

Who Is Jesus?

The first half of this chapter focuses on the question: What defiles a person? The Pharisees said that eating without washing your hands defiles you. By this they meant spiritual defilement, not the germs we would worry about today.

Jesus had a different answer. You are not defiled by what goes into your mouth, but by what comes out. The evil actions and words that defile us come from our hearts.

As we've noted before, Jesus hates hypocrisy. He knew how far from God the Pharisees were. He knew their worship was in vain because God did not accept it. They were dishonoring God by their teaching and their inconsistency.

The next section of this chapter is harder to understand. Why did Jesus delay answering this woman's request for Him to heal her daughter? He had earlier answered the requests of other Gentiles.

Was it a test? Was He trying to see if she genuinely believed? It is hard to say, but eventually He honored her humble faith and answered her request.

For us, too, there may be times when God seems not to hear us. If this happens, let's take this woman as an example and just pray more earnestly. God does hear us and wants what is best for us.

To Think About

1. Do you think Jesus was too hard on the Pharisees? Explain your answer.

2. Why do you think teaching the commands of men as spiritual doctrine is such a bad thing?

3. Can you think of times when you have defiled yourself by things you have done or said? What can you do to avoid such times?

4. In what ways was the Canaanite woman's answer a good one?

Lord, cleanse my heart of any wickedness and sin, so only pure thoughts, deeds, and words come from it.

JESUS IS ... a King who knows the hearts of people.

Who Is Jesus?

I, the LORD, have called You in righteousness, and will hold Your hand; I will keep You and give You as a covenant to the people, as a light to the Gentiles, To open blind eyes, to bring out prisoners from the prison, those who sit in darkness from the prison house. Isaiah 42:6–7, NKJV

READ MATTHEW 16

The Pharisees and Sadducees Demand Signs

[1] The Pharisees and Sadducees came, and testing him, asked him to show them a sign from heaven.

[2] But he answered them, "When it is evening, you say, 'It will be fair weather, for the sky is red.'

[3] In the morning, 'It will be foul weather today, for the sky is red and threatening.' Hypocrites! You know how to discern the appearance of the sky, but you can't discern the signs of the times!

[4] An evil and adulterous generation seeks after a sign, and there will be no sign

given to it, except the sign of the prophet Jonah." He left them, and departed.

The Leaven of the Pharisees and Sadducees

⁵ The disciples came to the other side and had forgotten to take bread.

⁶ Jesus said to them, "Take heed and beware of the yeast of the Pharisees and Sadducees."

⁷ They reasoned among themselves, saying, "We brought no bread."

⁸ Jesus, perceiving it, said, "Why do you reason among yourselves, you of little faith, 'because you have brought no bread?'

⁹ Don't you yet perceive, neither remember the five loaves for the five thousand, and how many baskets you took up?

¹⁰ Nor the seven loaves for the four thousand, and how many baskets you took up?

¹¹ How is it that you don't perceive that I didn't speak to you concerning bread? But beware of the yeast of the Pharisees and Sadducees."

¹² Then they understood that he didn't tell them to beware of the yeast of bread, but of the teaching of the Pharisees and Sadducees.

Peter Confesses Jesus as the Christ

¹³ Now when Jesus came into the parts of Caesarea Philippi, he asked his disciples, saying, "Who do men say that I, the Son of Man, am?"

¹⁴ They said, "Some say John the Baptizer, some, Elijah, and others, Jeremiah, or one of the prophets."

¹⁵ He said to them, "But who do you say that I am?"

¹⁶ Simon Peter answered, "You are the Christ, the Son of the living God."

¹⁷ Jesus answered him, "Blessed are you, Simon Bar Jonah, for flesh and blood has not revealed this to you, but my Father who is in heaven.

¹⁸ I also tell you that you are Peter, and on this rock I will build my assembly, and the gates of Hades will not prevail against it.

¹⁹ I will give to you the keys of the Kingdom of Heaven, and whatever you bind on earth will have been bound in heaven; and whatever you release on earth will have been released in heaven."

²⁰ Then he commanded the disciples that they should tell no one that he was Jesus the Christ.

Jesus Foretells His Death and Resurrection

²¹ From that time, Jesus began to show his disciples that he must go to Jerusalem and suffer many things from the elders, chief priests, and scribes, and be killed, and the third day be raised up.

²² Peter took him aside, and began to rebuke him, saying, "Far be it from you, Lord! This will never be done to you."

²³ But he turned, and said to Peter, "Get behind me, Satan! You are a stumbling block to me, for you are not setting your mind on the things of God, but on the things of men."

Take Up Your Cross and Follow Jesus

²⁴ Then Jesus said to his disciples, "If anyone desires to come after me, let him deny himself, and take up his cross, and follow me.

²⁵ For whoever desires to save his life will lose it, and whoever will lose his life for my sake will find it.

²⁶ For what will it profit a man, if he gains the whole world, and forfeits his life? Or what will a man give in exchange for his life?

²⁷ For the Son of Man will come in the glory of his Father with his angels, and then he will render to everyone according to his deeds.

²⁸ Most certainly I tell you, there are some standing here who will in no way taste of death, until they see the Son of Man coming in his Kingdom."

Who Is Jesus?

As you would expect, a lot of talk about Jesus was floating around Palestine. Some people thought He was one of the Old Testament prophets who had become alive again, or perhaps even John the Baptist.

Jesus didn't seem to worry about who other people thought He was, but He did want to know what His disciples thought. Peter, the outspoken one, was the first to answer: "You are the Christ, the Son of the living God."

Jesus complimented Peter on his answer. This may have

made Peter feel important, but it didn't take long for the bubble to burst. When Jesus tried to explain to the disciples that He would soon be killed, Peter took Him aside and tried to correct Him. Jesus told him in no uncertain terms that his thoughts were from Satan, not from God.

In this same context, Jesus explained to the disciples that dying for God is not a lost cause. It is worse to refuse to die for God. In fact, real death, which the Bible calls the second death, is what counts. People can escape persecution by refusing to serve God, but they will pay for it at the judgment when they face eternal death.

To Think About

1. How was the teaching of the Pharisees like leaven?

2. Peter knew the right answer to Jesus' question about who Jesus was, but he didn't seem to understand what it meant. How can you tell?

3. Does the last part of this chapter teach that Jesus requires each of us to die a martyr's death? Explain your answer.

Lord, I know you are the Son of the living God. Help me to live for you and be willing to die for you.

JESUS IS ... the Christ, the Son of the living God.

Who Is Jesus?

Now the glory of the LORD rested on Mount Sinai, and the cloud covered it six days. And on the seventh day He called to Moses out of the midst of the cloud. The sight of the glory of the LORD was like a consuming fire on the top of the mountain in the eyes of the children of Israel. Exodus 24:16–17, NKJV

READ MATTHEW 17

The Transfiguration

¹ After six days, Jesus took with him Peter, James, and John his brother, and brought them up into a high mountain by themselves.

² He was transfigured before them. His face shone like the sun, and his garments became as white as the light.

³ Behold, Moses and Elijah appeared to them talking with him.

⁴ Peter answered, and said to Jesus, "Lord, it is good for us to be here. If you want, let's make three tents here: one for you, one for Moses, and one for Elijah."

⁵ While he was still speaking, behold, a bright cloud overshadowed them. Behold, a voice

came out of the cloud, saying, "This is my beloved Son, in whom I am well pleased. Listen to him."

⁶ When the disciples heard it, they fell on their faces, and were very afraid.

⁷ Jesus came and touched them and said, "Get up, and don't be afraid."

⁸ Lifting up their eyes, they saw no one, except Jesus alone.

⁹ As they were coming down from the mountain, Jesus commanded them, saying, "Don't tell anyone what you saw, until the Son of Man has risen from the dead."

¹⁰ His disciples asked him, saying, "Then why do the scribes say that Elijah must come first?"

¹¹ Jesus answered them, "Elijah indeed comes first, and will restore all things,

¹² but I tell you that Elijah has come already, and they didn't recognize him, but did to him whatever they wanted to. Even so the Son of Man will also suffer by them."

¹³ Then the disciples understood that he spoke to them of John the Baptizer.

Jesus Heals a Boy with a Demon

¹⁴ When they came to the multitude, a man came to him, kneeling down to him, and saying,

¹⁵ "Lord, have mercy on my son, for he is epileptic, and suffers grievously; for he often falls into the fire, and often into the water.

¹⁶ So I brought him to your disciples, and they could not cure him."

¹⁷ Jesus answered, "Faithless and perverse generation! How long will I be with you? How long will I bear with you? Bring him here to me."

¹⁸ Jesus rebuked him, the demon went out of him, and the boy was cured from that hour.

¹⁹ Then the disciples came to Jesus privately, and said, "Why weren't we able to cast it out?"

²⁰ He said to them, "Because of your unbelief. For most certainly I tell you, if you have faith as a grain of mustard seed, you will tell this mountain, 'Move from here to there,' and it will move; and nothing will be impossible for you.

²¹ But this kind doesn't go out except by prayer and fasting."

Jesus Again Foretells Death, Resurrection

²² While they were staying in Galilee, Jesus said to them, "The Son of Man is about to be delivered up into the hands of men,

²³ and they will kill him, and the third day he will be raised up." They were exceedingly sorry.

The Temple Tax

²⁴ When they had come to Capernaum, those who collected the didrachma coins came to

Peter, and said, "Doesn't your teacher pay the didrachma?"

²⁵ He said, "Yes." When he came into the house, Jesus anticipated him, saying, "What do you think, Simon? From whom do the kings of the earth receive toll or tribute? From their children, or from strangers?"

²⁶ Peter said to him, "From strangers." Jesus said to him, "Therefore the children are exempt.

²⁷ But, lest we cause them to stumble, go to the sea, cast a hook, and take up the first fish that comes up. When you have opened its mouth, you will find a stater coin. Take that, and give it to them for me and you."

Who Is Jesus?

Jesus came to earth as a man, even though He was also God. But once in a while His heavenly connections shone through, as if God just couldn't stay quiet about Him. This chapter shows one of those times.

Peter, James, and John were privileged to see Jesus' transformation as He spoke with Moses and Elijah. (Another Gospel adds that they were talking about His coming death.)

During this episode, the glory of God suddenly descended onto the mountaintop, and God spoke from the cloud.

Very few people have been privileged to see the Shekinah glory, as this shining cloud of God's presence is often called. But even fewer have had the privilege of hearing God's voice as well. I am sure the three disciples never forgot this experience.

This experience was a highlight of Jesus' earthly life. God probably granted this to give Him strength to face His death, which was on His mind during this time.

Although Jesus was God, He was also human and subject to fear and pain. It is impossible for us to picture the trauma of what He was facing, and the courage it took for Him to go through with it.

Jesus was faced with the realities of life as soon as He returned from the mountain, when a distraught man came to meet Him. He had brought his son to the disciples to be healed, but they couldn't do it. Jesus was likely tempted to wonder how they would get along without Him after He was gone. However, this did not stop Him from healing the child.

To Think About

1. Jesus had no one on earth He could confide in. There was no one who really understood Him or His mission. Why would the transfiguration experience have been an encouragement to Him?

2. It is hard for us to understand how Jesus could have been man and God at the same time, or how that would have affected Him. But during the latter part of His life, the human side of Him comes through more clearly. How do you see His humanity in this chapter?

3. What advice did Jesus give to the disciples to help them deal with difficult situations in the future, after He was no longer with them?

Thank you, Father, for a King like Jesus
who has my best interests at heart.

JESUS IS ... a King who has the Father's approval.

DAY 18

Who Is Jesus?

But now, thus says the LORD, who created you, O Jacob, and He who formed you, O Israel: Fear not, for I have redeemed you; I have called you by your name; you are Mine. When you pass through the waters, I will be with you; and through the rivers, they shall not overflow you. When you walk through the fire, you shall not be burned, nor shall the flame scorch you. Isaiah 43:1–2, NKJV

READ MATTHEW 18

Who Is the Greatest?

¹ In that hour the disciples came to Jesus, saying, "Who then is greatest in the Kingdom of Heaven?"

² Jesus called a little child to himself, and set him in the middle of them,

³ and said, "Most certainly I tell you, unless you turn, and become as little children, you will in no way enter into the Kingdom of Heaven.

⁴ Whoever therefore humbles himself as this little child, the same is the greatest in the Kingdom of Heaven.

⁵ Whoever receives one such little child in my name receives me,

⁶ but whoever causes one of these little ones who believe in me to stumble, it would be better for him that a huge millstone should be hung around his neck, and that he should be sunk in the depths of the sea.

Temptations to Sin

⁷ "Woe to the world because of occasions of stumbling! For it must be that the occasions come, but woe to that person through whom the occasion comes!

⁸ If your hand or your foot causes you to stumble, cut it off, and cast it from you. It is better for you to enter into life maimed or crippled, rather than having two hands or two feet to be cast into the eternal fire.

⁹ If your eye causes you to stumble, pluck it out, and cast it from you. It is better for you to enter into life with one eye, rather than having two eyes to be cast into the Gehenna of fire.

The Parable of the Lost Sheep

¹⁰ See that you don't despise one of these little ones, for I tell you that in heaven their angels always see the face of my Father who is in heaven.

¹¹ For the Son of Man came to save that which was lost.

¹² "What do you think? If a man has one hundred sheep, and one of them goes astray, doesn't he leave the ninety-nine, go to the mountains, and seek that which has gone astray?

¹³ If he finds it, most certainly I tell you, he rejoices over it more than over the ninety-nine which have not gone astray.

¹⁴ Even so it is not the will of your Father who is in heaven that one of these little ones should perish.

If Your Brother Sins Against You

¹⁵ "If your brother sins against you, go, show him his fault between you and him alone. If he listens to you, you have gained back your brother.

¹⁶ But if he doesn't listen, take one or two more with you, that at the mouth of two or three witnesses every word may be established.

¹⁷ If he refuses to listen to them, tell it to the assembly. If he refuses to hear the assembly also, let him be to you as a Gentile or a tax collector.

¹⁸ Most certainly I tell you, whatever things you bind on earth will have been bound in heaven, and whatever things you release on earth will have been released in heaven.

¹⁹ Again, assuredly I tell you, that if two of you will agree on earth concerning anything that they will ask, it will be done for them by my Father who is in heaven.

²⁰ For where two or three are gathered together in my name, there I am in the middle of them."

The Parable of the Unforgiving Servant

²¹ Then Peter came and said to him, "Lord, how often shall my brother sin against me, and I forgive him? Until seven times?"

²² Jesus said to him, "I don't tell you until seven times, but, until seventy times seven.

²³ Therefore the Kingdom of Heaven is like a certain king, who wanted to reconcile accounts with his servants.

²⁴ When he had begun to reconcile, one was brought to him who owed him ten thousand talents.

²⁵ But because he couldn't pay, his lord commanded him to be sold, with his wife, his children, and all that he had, and payment to be made.

²⁶ The servant therefore fell down and knelt before him, saying, 'Lord, have patience with me, and I will repay you all!'

²⁷ The lord of that servant, being moved with compassion, released him, and forgave him the debt.

²⁸ "But that servant went out, and found one of his fellow servants, who owed him one hundred denarii, and he grabbed him, and took him by the throat, saying, 'Pay me what you owe!'

²⁹ "So his fellow servant fell down at his feet and begged him, saying, 'Have patience with me, and I will repay you!'

³⁰ He would not, but went and cast him into prison, until he should pay back that which was due.

³¹ So when his fellow servants saw what was done, they were exceedingly sorry,

and came and told their lord all that was done.

³² Then his lord called him in, and said to him, 'You wicked servant! I forgave you all that debt, because you begged me.

³³ Shouldn't you also have had mercy on your fellow servant, even as I had mercy on you?'

³⁴ His lord was angry, and delivered him to the tormentors, until he should pay all that was due to him.

³⁵ So my heavenly Father will also do to you, if you don't each forgive your brother from your hearts for his misdeeds."

Who Is Jesus?

Who is the greatest? That question has caused a lot of grief. Wanting to be the greatest is a problem most people have, and the disciples were no exception. It seems they were constantly vying for an important position in the earthly kingdom they expected Jesus to set up.

Jesus understood all this. He also understood what the disciples needed to learn. So He called for a little child to use as an example and talked to them about humility.

When people are concerned about their own greatness and position, they tend to misuse other people who get in their way. In the rest of this chapter, Jesus went on to talk to the disciples about this.

You can sin against little children by destroying their faith in God. You can be an offense to others by tempting them to sin, or they can cause the offense by tempting you to sin. In any case, Jesus makes it very clear that it is better to take drastic action to avoid sinning than to take a chance on missing heaven.

Jesus then talked about despising others, especially people

we might be tempted to consider inferior to us. We should seek to help others grow in their faith rather than writing them off. We even have a responsibility to help those who mistreat us.

The final story in the chapter summarizes all this. As a Christian, you have been forgiven much. Are you now willing to forgive others?

To Think About

1. In what ways are little children a good illustration of humility?

2. Why is the desire for greatness such a problem? What can it do to you?

3. Why might it be just as important to let a brother know that he has sinned against you as it is for you to apologize if you have sinned against him? Which do you find easiest to do?

4. What warning did Jesus give to those who do not forgive others even though they have been forgiven much?

Lord, help me not to sin against you by the way I treat others, especially weaker ones I come in contact with.

JESUS IS ... a King who understands the value of human relationships.

DAY 19

Who Is Jesus?

I will raise up for them a Prophet like you from among
their brethren, and will put My words in His mouth,
and He shall speak to them all that I command Him.
Deuteronomy 18:18, NKJV

READ MATTHEW 19

Teaching About Divorce

¹ When Jesus had finished these words, he departed from Galilee, and came
into the borders of Judea beyond the Jordan.

² Great multitudes followed him, and he healed them there.

³ Pharisees came to him, testing him, and saying, "Is it lawful for a man to divorce his wife for any reason?"

⁴ He answered, "Haven't you read that he who made them from the beginning
made them male and female,

⁵ and said, 'For this cause a man shall leave his father and mother, and shall

be joined to his wife; and the two shall become one flesh?'

⁶ So that they are no more two, but one flesh. What therefore God has joined together, don't let man tear apart."

⁷ They asked him, "Why then did Moses command us to give her a certificate of divorce, and divorce her?"

⁸ He said to them, "Moses, because of the hardness of your hearts, allowed you to divorce your wives, but from the beginning it has not been so.

⁹ I tell you that whoever divorces his wife, except for sexual immorality, and marries another, commits adultery; and he who marries her when she is divorced commits adultery."

¹⁰ His disciples said to him, "If this is the case of the man with his wife, it is not expedient to marry."

¹¹ But he said to them, "Not all men can receive this saying, but those to whom it is given.

¹² For there are eunuchs who were born that way from their mother's womb, and there are eunuchs who were made eunuchs by men; and there are eunuchs who made themselves eunuchs for the Kingdom of Heaven's sake. He who is able to receive it, let him receive it."

Let the Children Come to Me

¹³ Then little children were brought to him, that he should lay his hands on them and pray; and the disciples rebuked them.

¹⁴ But Jesus said, "Allow the little children, and don't forbid them to come to me; for the Kingdom of Heaven belongs to ones like these."

¹⁵ He laid his hands on them, and departed from there.

The Rich Young Man

¹⁶ Behold, one came to him and said, "Good teacher, what good thing shall I do, that I may have eternal life?"

¹⁷ He said to him, "Why do you call me good? No one is good but one, that is, God. But if you want to enter into life, keep the commandments."

¹⁸ He said to him, "Which ones?" Jesus said, " 'You shall not murder.' 'You shall

not commit adultery.' 'You shall not steal.' 'You shall not offer false testimony.'

¹⁹ 'Honor your father and your mother.' And, 'You shall love your neighbor as yourself.' "

²⁰ The young man said to him, "All these things I have observed from my youth. What do I still lack?"

²¹ Jesus said to him, "If you want to be perfect, go, sell what you have, and give to the poor, and you will have treasure in heaven; and come, follow me."

²² But when the young man heard the saying, he went away sad, for he was one who had great possessions.

²³ Jesus said to his disciples, "Most certainly I say to you, a rich man will enter into the Kingdom of Heaven with difficulty.

²⁴ Again I tell you, it is easier for a camel to go through a needle's eye, than for a rich man to enter into God's Kingdom."

²⁵ When the disciples heard it, they were exceedingly astonished, saying, "Who then can be saved?"

²⁶ Looking at them, Jesus said, "With men this is impossible, but with God all things are possible."

²⁷ Then Peter answered, "Behold, we have left everything, and followed you. What then will we have?"

²⁸ Jesus said to them, "Most certainly I tell you that you who have followed me, in the regeneration when the Son of Man will sit on the throne of his glory, you also will sit on twelve thrones, judging the twelve tribes of Israel.

²⁹ Everyone who has left houses, or brothers, or sisters, or father, or mother, or wife, or children, or lands, for my name's sake, will receive one hundred times, and will inherit eternal life.

³⁰ But many will be last who are first; and first who are last.

Who Is Jesus?

This chapter mainly discusses two unrelated subjects. The Pharisees wanted to know what Jesus had to say about divorce. Some of the rabbis taught that a man could divorce his wife for almost any reason. Other rabbis taught that he could do so for only a few specific reasons.

Jesus, however, left room for divorce only in the case of immorality, which was tighter than any of the rabbis taught. But then He took the subject a step further and stated that if a man divorced his wife and remarried, he committed adultery. And if he married a divorced woman he committed adultery.

This was new teaching for the Jews, and even the disciples objected. Jesus told them that the only way around this principle was to remain single.

The other main passage, starting at verse sixteen, centers on the question: "What good thing can I do to have eternal life?"

Jesus told the young man, "Obey the commandments." The young man wanted a more specific answer, so Jesus mentioned some of them. The young man said he had kept all these, but wondered if there was something else he should do.

Jesus touched on the one point that the young man felt he could not do—place his possessions under God's control.

God wants His people to serve Him from the heart. Merely trying to obey certain commandments without actually yielding our will to Him is not enough. We do not earn salvation by doing good works. I think Jesus was trying to show him this, but he didn't understand. We are saved by surrendering our life to God and living in obedience to Him.

To Think About

1. Why might the disciples have felt it would be better not

to get married when Jesus told them His position on divorce and remarriage?

2. Why might it be so hard for a rich person to enter the kingdom of heaven?

3. What do you have that you would find hard to give up if God asked you to?

Lord, I pray for grace and strength to follow you, even if you ask hard things of me.

JESUS IS ... a King
who is not afraid to ask
hard things of us.

DAY 20

Who Is Jesus?

After these things I looked, and behold, a great multitude
which no one could number, of all nations, tribes,
peoples, and tongues, standing before the throne and
before the Lamb, clothed with white robes, with palm
branches in their hands, and crying out with a loud voice,
saying, Salvation belongs to our God who sits on the
throne, and to the Lamb! Revelation 7:9, 10, NKJV

READ MATTHEW 20

Laborers in the Vineyard

[1] "For the Kingdom of Heaven is like a man who was the master of a household, who went out early in the morning to hire laborers for his vineyard.

[2] When he had agreed with the laborers for a denarius a day, he sent
them into his vineyard.

[3] He went out about the third hour, and saw others standing idle in
the marketplace.

[4] He said to them, 'You also go into the vineyard, and whatever is right
I will give you.' So they went their way.

⁵ Again he went out about the sixth and the ninth hour, and did likewise.

⁶ About the eleventh hour he went out, and found others standing idle. He said to them, 'Why do you stand here all day idle?'

⁷ "They said to him, 'Because no one has hired us.' "He said to them, 'You also go into the vineyard, and you will receive whatever is right.'

⁸ When evening had come, the lord of the vineyard said to his manager, 'Call the laborers and pay them their wages, beginning from the last to the first.'

⁹ "When those who were hired at about the eleventh hour came, they each received a denarius.

¹⁰ When the first came, they supposed that they would receive more; and they likewise each received a denarius.

¹¹ When they received it, they murmured against the master of the household,

¹² saying, 'These last have spent one hour, and you have made them equal to us, who have borne the burden of the day and the scorching heat!'

¹³ "But he answered one of them, 'Friend, I am doing you no wrong. Didn't you agree with me for a denarius?

¹⁴ Take that which is yours, and go your way. It is my desire to give to this last just as much as to you.

¹⁵ Isn't it lawful for me to do what I want to with what I own? Or is your eye evil, because I am good?'

¹⁶ So the last will be first, and the first last. For many are called, but few are chosen."

Jesus Foretells His Death a Third Time

¹⁷ As Jesus was going up to Jerusalem, he took the twelve disciples aside, and on the way he said to them,

¹⁸ "Behold, we are going up to Jerusalem, and the Son of Man will be delivered to the chief priests and scribes, and they will condemn him to death,

¹⁹ and will hand him over to the Gentiles to mock, to scourge, and to crucify; and the third day he will be raised up."

A Mother's Request

²⁰ Then the mother of the sons of Zebedee came to him with her sons, kneeling and asking a certain thing of him.

²¹ He said to her, "What do you want?" She said to him, "Command that these, my two sons, may sit, one on your right hand, and one on your left hand, in your Kingdom."

²² But Jesus answered, "You don't know what you are asking. Are you able to drink the cup that I am about to drink, and be baptized with the baptism that I am baptized with?" They said to him, "We are able."

²³ He said to them, "You will indeed drink my cup, and be baptized with the baptism that I am baptized with, but to sit on my right hand and on my left hand is not mine to give; but it is for whom it has been prepared by my Father."

²⁴ When the ten heard it, they were indignant with the two brothers.

²⁵ But Jesus summoned them, and said, "You know that the rulers of the nations lord it over them, and their great ones exercise authority over them.

²⁶ It shall not be so among you, but whoever desires to become great among you shall be your servant.

²⁷ Whoever desires to be first among you shall be your bondservant,

²⁸ even as the Son of Man came not to be served, but to serve, and to give his life as a ransom for many."

Jesus Heals Two Blind Men

²⁹ As they went out from Jericho, a great multitude followed him.

³⁰ Behold, two blind men sitting by the road, when they heard that Jesus was passing by, cried out, "Lord, have mercy on us, you son of David!"

³¹ The multitude rebuked them, telling them that they should be quiet, but they cried out even more, "Lord, have mercy on us, you son of David!"

^{32} Jesus stood still, and called them, and asked, "What do you want me to do for you?"

^{33} They told him, "Lord, that our eyes may be opened."

^{34} Jesus, being moved with compassion, touched their eyes; and immediately their eyes received their sight, and they followed him.

Who Is Jesus?

What is the kingdom of heaven like? Jesus told the story of the laborers in the vineyard to answer that question. Notice that this discussion is tied to the last verse of chapter nineteen, where Jesus said that "many who are first will be last, and the last first."

Jesus apparently saw that some in the crowd didn't understand what this statement meant, so He continued His discourse. At the end of the story, in verse sixteen, He repeated His statement but added to it: "Many are called, but few are chosen."

So, what *is* the kingdom of heaven like? It is like a farmer who needs workers to pick grapes. If you lived in Israel at that time and needed work, you went to the marketplace so local farmers would hire you for the day.

In this case, the farmer hired all the people who wanted work, but he still needed more workers. So several times during the day he hired more people.

At the end of the day he paid everyone the same wage, whether they had worked all day, part of the day, or even just the last hour of the day.

What does this tell us? Several things. First, the kingdom of heaven has room for all. No one is turned away. Also, all those who enter the kingdom of heaven are treated equally. And in many cases, they are rewarded far above what they are worthy of.

Why are the last first and the first last? Because the priorities of the kingdom are not like anything we are used to. You won't be the most important because you have served the longest, the hardest, or with the most skill.

But they didn't get it. Soon after this, James and John and their mother saw a chance to speak to Jesus in private. They wanted to be assured that they would have the best seats in Jesus' kingdom. This really upset the other ten disciples, probably because they wanted the best seats too.

Jesus saw that it was time for another lesson . . .

To Think About

1. Why did the workers who were hired in the morning expect that the landowner would pay them more than he had promised?

2. Why might God treat everyone in the kingdom of heaven the same even though they didn't accomplish the same amount of work? Explain your answer.

3. Jesus had just made it clear in yesterday's reading that the disciples would receive a reward for

their faithfulness. What do you suppose motivated James and John and their mother to ask for more special privileges?

4. What is another way that the last will be first and the first last according to verses 25-28?

Lord, take away the desire for greatness from my heart. Help me to serve you for who you are, rather than for a desire for rewards.

JESUS IS ... a King who welcomes everyone into His kingdom on the same basis.

Who Is Jesus?

Rejoice greatly, O daughter of Zion! Shout, O daughter of Jerusalem! Behold, your King is coming to you; He is just and having salvation, lowly and riding on a donkey, a colt, the foal of a donkey. Zechariah 9:9, NKJV

READ MATTHEW 21

The Triumphal Entry

¹ When they came near to Jerusalem, and came to Bethsphage, to the Mount of Olives, then Jesus sent two disciples,

² saying to them, "Go into the village that is opposite you, and immediately you will find a donkey tied, and a colt with her. Untie them, and bring them to me.

³ If anyone says anything to you, you shall say, 'The Lord needs them,' and immediately he will send them."

⁴ All this was done, that it might be fulfilled which was spoken through the prophet, saying,

⁵ "Tell the daughter of Zion, behold, your King comes to you, humble, and riding on a donkey, on a colt, the foal of a donkey."

⁶ The disciples went, and did just as Jesus commanded them,

⁷ and brought the donkey and the colt, and laid their clothes on them; and he sat on them.

⁸ A very great multitude spread their clothes on the road. Others cut branches from the trees, and spread them on the road.

⁹ The multitudes who went in front of him, and those who followed, kept shouting, "Hosanna to the son of David! Blessed is he who comes in the name of the Lord! Hosanna in the highest!"

¹⁰ When he had come into Jerusalem, all the city was stirred up, saying, "Who is this?"

¹¹ The multitudes said, "This is the prophet, Jesus, from Nazareth of Galilee."

Jesus Cleanses the Temple

¹² Jesus entered into the temple of God, and drove out all of those who sold and bought in the temple, and overthrew the money changers' tables and the seats of those who sold the doves.

¹³ He said to them, "It is written, 'My house shall be called a house of prayer,' but you have made it a den of robbers!"

¹⁴ The blind and the lame came to him in the temple, and he healed them.

¹⁵ But when the chief priests and the scribes saw the wonderful things that he did, and the children who were crying in the temple and saying, "Hosanna to the son of David!" they were indignant,

¹⁶ and said to him, "Do you hear what these are saying?" Jesus said to them, "Yes. Did you never read, 'Out of the mouth of babes and nursing babies you have perfected praise?'"

¹⁷ He left them, and went out of the city to Bethany, and camped there.

Jesus Curses the Fig Tree

¹⁸ Now in the morning, as he returned to the city, he was hungry.

¹⁹ Seeing a fig tree by the road, he came to it, and found nothing on it but

leaves. He said to it, "Let there be no fruit from you forever!" Immediately the fig tree withered away.

²⁰ When the disciples saw it, they marveled, saying, "How did the fig tree immediately wither away?"

²¹ Jesus answered them, "Most certainly I tell you, if you have faith, and don't doubt, you will not only do what was done to the fig tree, but even if you told this mountain, 'Be taken up and cast into the sea,' it would be done.

²² All things, whatever you ask in prayer, believing, you will receive."

The Authority of Jesus Challenged

²³ When he had come into the temple, the chief priests and the elders of the people came to him as he was teaching, and said, "By what authority do you do these things? Who gave you this authority?"

²⁴ Jesus answered them, "I also will ask you one question, which if you tell me, I likewise will tell you by what authority I do these things.

²⁵ The baptism of John, where was it from? From heaven or from men?" They reasoned with themselves, saying, "If we say, 'From heaven,' he will ask us, 'Why then did you not believe him?'

²⁶ But if we say, 'From men,' we fear the multitude, for all hold John as a prophet."

²⁷ They answered Jesus, and said, "We don't know." He also said to them, "Neither will I tell you by what authority I do these things.

The Parable of the Two Sons

²⁸ But what do you think? A man had two sons, and he came to the first, and said, 'Son, go work today in my vineyard.'

²⁹ He answered, 'I will not,' but afterward he changed his mind, and went.

³⁰ He came to the second, and said the same thing. He answered, 'I'm going, sir,' but he didn't go.

³¹ Which of the two did the will of his father?" They said to him, "The first." Jesus said to them, "Most certainly I tell you that the tax collectors and the prostitutes are entering into God's Kingdom before you.

³² For John came to you in the way of righteousness, and you didn't believe

him, but the tax collectors and the prostitutes believed him. When you saw it, you didn't even repent afterward, that you might believe him.

The Parable of the Tenants

³³ "Hear another parable. There was a man who was a master of a household, who planted a vineyard, set a hedge about it, dug a wine press in it, built a tower, leased it out to farmers, and went into another country.

³⁴ When the season for the fruit came near, he sent his servants to the farmers, to receive his fruit.

³⁵ The farmers took his servants, beat one, killed another, and stoned another.

³⁶ Again, he sent other servants more than the first: and they treated them the same way.

³⁷ But afterward he sent to them his son, saying, 'They will respect my son.'

³⁸ But the farmers, when they saw the son, said among themselves, 'This is the heir. Come, let's kill him, and seize his inheritance.'

³⁹ So they took him, and threw him out of the vineyard, and killed him.

⁴⁰ When therefore the lord of the vineyard comes, what will he do to those farmers?"

⁴¹ They told him, "He will miserably destroy those miserable men, and will lease out the vineyard to other farmers, who will give him the fruit in its season."

⁴² Jesus said to them, "Did you never read in the Scriptures, 'The stone which the builders rejected, the same was made the head of the corner. This was from the Lord. It is marvelous in our eyes?'

⁴³ "Therefore I tell you, God's Kingdom will be taken away from you, and will be given to a nation producing its fruit.

⁴⁴ He who falls on this stone will be broken to pieces, but on whomever it will fall, it will scatter him as dust."

⁴⁵ When the chief priests and the Pharisees heard his parables, they perceived that he spoke about them.

⁴⁶ When they sought to seize him, they feared the multitudes, because they considered him to be a prophet.

Who Is Jesus?

Matthew linked Jesus' life with Old Testament prophecy whenever he could. In this chapter he quoted from Zechariah 9:9 and showed how Jesus fulfilled this prophecy. Again, the point was that Jesus was a King. He was the Messiah the Jews had long anticipated.

After arriving in Jerusalem, riding on a donkey's colt, Jesus went to the temple. The outer court resembled a marketplace more than a place of worship. Jesus, of course, had seen this many times before, but this time He did something about it. He took a whip and drove out the animals, knocked over the tables, and chased out the merchants.

It appears that once the outer court was empty, people swarmed in to be healed. The priests were very upset, of course. But Jesus was a King, even though they didn't know it, and He had the right to reclaim God's house for its true purpose.

The next day the priests and elders confronted Jesus again and demanded that He tell them where He got his authority. Jesus, in turn, told them two stories aimed at their rejection of God's authority.

The priests now had their answer. Jesus was saying that His authority came from God, and they were rejecting God by rejecting Him.

The anger of the Jewish leaders was ready to boil over. They would have arrested Jesus right then and there, but they were afraid it would create a riot.

But the end of the confrontation was at hand.

To Think About

1. Jesus instigated the triumphal entry, but the people were ready to participate. What did they do that shows this?

2. How do you think the cleansing of the temple reinforced the people's belief that Jesus was a King?

3. How did Jesus challenge the authority of the priests and the Pharisees?

Lord, you are our King. Help us to
serve you as you deserve to be served.

JESUS IS...
a King with authority.

DAY 22

Who Is Jesus?

And now, Israel, what does the LORD your God require of you, but to fear the LORD your God, to walk in all His ways and to love Him, to serve the LORD your God with all your heart and with all your soul, and to keep the commandments of the LORD and His statutes which I command you today for your good? Deuteronomy 10:12, 13, NKJV

READ MATTHEW 22

The Parable of the Wedding Feast

¹ Jesus answered and spoke to them again in parables, saying,

² "The Kingdom of Heaven is like a certain king, who made a marriage feast for his son,

³ and sent out his servants to call those who were invited to the marriage feast, but they would not come.

⁴ Again he sent out other servants, saying, 'Tell those who are invited, "Behold, I have prepared my dinner. My cattle and my fatlings are killed, and all things are ready. Come to the marriage feast!"'

⁵ But they made light of it, and went their ways, one to his own farm, another

to his merchandise,

⁶ and the rest grabbed his servants, and treated them shamefully, and killed them.

⁷ When the king heard that, he was angry, and sent his armies, destroyed those murderers, and burned their city.

⁸ "Then he said to his servants, 'The wedding is ready, but those who were invited weren't worthy.

⁹ Go therefore to the intersections of the highways, and as many as you may find, invite to the marriage feast.'

¹⁰ Those servants went out into the highways, and gathered together as many as they found, both bad and good. The wedding was filled with guests.

¹¹ But when the king came in to see the guests, he saw there a man who didn't have on wedding clothing,

¹² and he said to him, 'Friend, how did you come in here not wearing wedding clothing?' He was speechless.

¹³ Then the king said to the servants, 'Bind him hand and foot, take him away, and throw him into the outer darkness. That is where the weeping and grinding of teeth will be.'

¹⁴ For many are called, but few chosen."

Paying Taxes to Caesar

¹⁵ Then the Pharisees went and took counsel how they might entrap him in his talk.

¹⁶ They sent their disciples to him, along with the Herodians, saying, "Teacher, we know that you are honest, and teach the way of God in truth, no matter whom you teach, for you aren't partial to anyone.

¹⁷ Tell us therefore, what do you think? Is it lawful to pay taxes to Caesar, or not?"

¹⁸ But Jesus perceived their wickedness, and said, "Why do you test me, you hypocrites?

¹⁹ Show me the tax money." They brought to him a denarius.

²⁰ He asked them, "Whose is this image and inscription?"

²¹ They said to him, "Caesar's." Then he said to them, "Give therefore to Caesar the things that are Caesar's, and to God the things that are God's."

²² When they heard it, they marveled, and left him, and went away.

Sadducees Ask About the Resurrection

²³ On that day Sadducees (those who say that there is no resurrection) came to him. They asked him,

²⁴ saying, "Teacher, Moses said, 'If a man dies, having no children, his brother shall marry his wife, and raise up offspring for his brother.'

²⁵ Now there were with us seven brothers. The first married and died, and having no offspring left his wife to his brother.

²⁶ In the same way, the second also, and the third, to the seventh.

²⁷ After them all, the woman died.

²⁸ In the resurrection therefore, whose wife will she be of the seven? For they all had her."

²⁹ But Jesus answered them, "You are mistaken, not knowing the Scriptures, nor the power of God.

³⁰ For in the resurrection they neither marry, nor are given in marriage, but are like God's angels in heaven.

³¹ But concerning the resurrection of the dead, haven't you read that which was spoken to you by God, saying,

³² 'I am the God of Abraham, and the God of Isaac, and the God of Jacob?' God is not the God of the dead, but of the living."

³³ When the multitudes heard it, they were astonished at his teaching.

The Great Commandment

³⁴ But the Pharisees, when they heard that he had silenced the Sadducees, gathered themselves together.

³⁵ One of them, a lawyer, asked him a question, testing him.

³⁶ "Teacher, which is the greatest commandment in the law?"

³⁷ Jesus said to him, "'You shall love the Lord your God with all your heart, with all your soul, and with all your mind.'

³⁸ This is the first and great commandment.

³⁹ A second likewise is this, 'You shall love your neighbor as yourself.'

⁴⁰ The whole law and the prophets depend on these two commandments."

Whose Son Is the Christ?

[41] Now while the Pharisees were gathered together, Jesus asked them a question,

[42] saying, "What do you think of the Christ? Whose son is he?" They said to him, "Of David."

[43] He said to them, "How then does David in the Spirit call him Lord, saying,

[44] 'The Lord said to my Lord, sit on my right hand, until I make your enemies a footstool for your feet?'

[45] "If then David calls him Lord, how is he his son?"

[46] No one was able to answer him a word, neither did any man dare ask him any more questions from that day forward.

Who Is Jesus?

We should always pay careful attention when Jesus starts a conversation by saying, "The kingdom of heaven is like . . ." In this case, the story is about a king who made a wedding feast for his son. But no one came. Even today, this would be considered a serious insult. In Jesus' time, it was even more so.

The story is a parable about God and the Jewish people. The Jews had killed many of God's prophets over the years, and both Jews and Gentiles would continue to do the same to the followers of Christ in the years to come.

The invited guests paid dearly for rejecting the king's invitation. But this didn't change the king's plan to host a "wedding feast" for his son. The people who did come to the feast had never expected to be invited by a king. Not in their wildest dreams.

In the same way, the citizens of the kingdom of heaven are often people whom society has written off or considers worthless.

Later in the chapter we read about a lawyer who asked Jesus which commandment in the Law was the greatest. Jesus told him that the greatest commandment was to love God, and the second greatest commandment was to love your neighbor. These two commands were so important, according to Jesus, that they summarized all the Old Testament laws.

Jesus repeated this various times throughout His ministry, and the rest of the New Testament verifies the importance of love in God's sight.

To Think About

1. The Pharisees knew that Jesus was talking about them. Why is it such a great sin for people to reject God's invitation to them?

2. This chapter records several incidents where the Pharisees and Sadducees tried to outwit Jesus. But by the end of the chapter, they admitted defeat. Why?

3. In the book of Acts, it states that many of the priests became Christians. How might incidents like the ones in this chapter have helped the Pharisees and Sadducees turn to Jesus later?

Thank you, Father, for inviting me to the marriage feast of your Son. Help me to be a worthy citizen of the kingdom of heaven.

JESUS IS . . . a King who loves those who follow Him.

DAY 23

Who Is Jesus?

For the lips of a priest should keep knowledge, and people should seek the law from his mouth; for he is the messenger of the LORD of hosts. But you have departed from the way; you have caused many to stumble at the law. You have corrupted the covenant of Levi, says the LORD of hosts. Malachi 2:7–8, NKJV

READ MATTHEW 23

Seven Woes to the Scribes and Pharisees

¹ Then Jesus spoke to the multitudes and to his disciples,

² saying, "The scribes and the Pharisees sat on Moses' seat.

³ All things therefore whatever they tell you to observe, observe and do, but don't do their works; for they say, and don't do.

⁴ For they bind heavy burdens that are grievous to be borne, and lay them on men's shoulders; but they themselves will not lift a finger to help them.

⁵ But all their works they do to be seen by men. They make their phylacteries broad, enlarge the fringes of their garments,

⁶ and love the place of honor at feasts, the best seats in the synagogues,

⁷ the salutations in the marketplaces, and to be called 'Rabbi, Rabbi' by men.

⁸ But don't you be called 'Rabbi,' for one is your teacher, the Christ, and all of you are brothers.

⁹ Call no man on the earth your father, for one is your Father, he who is in heaven.

¹⁰ Neither be called masters, for one is your master, the Christ.

¹¹ But he who is greatest among you will be your servant.

¹² Whoever exalts himself will be humbled, and whoever humbles himself will be exalted.

¹³ "Woe to you, scribes and Pharisees, hypocrites! For you devour widows' houses, and as a pretense you make long prayers. Therefore you will receive greater condemnation.

¹⁴ "But woe to you, scribes and Pharisees, hypocrites! Because you shut up the Kingdom of Heaven against men; for you don't enter in yourselves, neither do you allow those who are entering in to enter.

¹⁵ Woe to you, scribes and Pharisees, hypocrites! For you travel around by sea and land to make one proselyte; and when he becomes one, you make him twice as much a son of Gehenna as yourselves.

¹⁶ "Woe to you, you blind guides, who say, 'Whoever swears by the temple, it is nothing; but whoever swears by the gold of the temple, he is obligated.'

¹⁷ You blind fools! For which is greater, the gold, or the temple that sanctifies the gold?

¹⁸ 'Whoever swears by the altar, it is nothing; but whoever swears by the gift that is on it, he is obligated?'

¹⁹ You blind fools! For which is greater, the gift, or the altar that sanctifies the gift?

²⁰ He therefore who swears by the altar, swears by it, and by everything on it.

²¹ He who swears by the temple, swears by it, and by him who has been living in it.

²² He who swears by heaven, swears by the throne of God, and by him who sits on it.

²³ "Woe to you, scribes and Pharisees, hypocrites! For you tithe mint, dill, and cumin, and have left undone the weightier matters of the law: justice, mercy, and faith. But you ought to have done these, and not to have left the other undone.

²⁴ You blind guides, who strain out a gnat, and swallow a camel!

²⁵ "Woe to you, scribes and Pharisees, hypocrites! For you clean the outside of

the cup and of the platter, but within they are full of extortion and unrighteousness.

²⁶ You blind Pharisee, first clean the inside of the cup and of the platter, that its outside may become clean also.

²⁷ "Woe to you, scribes and Pharisees, hypocrites! For you are like whitened tombs, which outwardly appear beautiful, but inwardly are full of dead men's bones, and of all uncleanness.

²⁸ Even so you also outwardly appear righteous to men, but inwardly you are full of hypocrisy and iniquity.

²⁹ "Woe to you, scribes and Pharisees, hypocrites! For you build the tombs of the prophets, and decorate the tombs of the righteous,

³⁰ and say, 'If we had lived in the days of our fathers, we wouldn't have been partakers with them in the blood of the prophets.'

³¹ Therefore you testify to yourselves that you are children of those who killed the prophets.

³² Fill up, then, the measure of your fathers.

³³ You serpents, you offspring of vipers, how will you escape the judgment of Gehenna?

³⁴ Therefore behold, I send to you prophets, wise men, and scribes. Some of them you will kill and crucify; and some of them you will scourge in your synagogues, and persecute from city to city;

³⁵ that on you may come all the righteous blood shed on the earth, from the blood of righteous Abel to the blood of Zachariah son of Barachiah, whom you killed between the sanctuary and the altar.

³⁶ Most certainly I tell you, all these things will come upon this generation.

Lament over Jerusalem

³⁷ "Jerusalem, Jerusalem, who kills the prophets, and stones those who are sent to her! How often I would have gathered your children together, even as a hen gathers her chicks under her wings, and you would not!

³⁸ Behold, your house is left to you desolate.

³⁹ For I tell you, you will not see me from now on, until you say, 'Blessed is he who comes in the name of the Lord!' "

Who Is Jesus?

The differences between Jesus and the scribes and Pharisees had been building for about three years, but this chapter was in many ways the climax. In fact, what Jesus said here may have clinched the determination of the Jewish leaders to kill Him. The events of this chapter took place during the last week of Jesus' life.

Jesus started in with a blistering description of the scribes and Pharisees. He denounced them as hypocrites of the worst order. Seven times He said, "Woe unto you, scribes and Pharisees . . ." Each time He followed the woe with an explanation.

Why did Jesus hate hypocrisy so much? When God's people are not what they pretend to be, they give people the wrong impression of God. They turn people against God. It seems Jesus was trying once again to get through to the scribes and Pharisees and show them how God felt about them.

The end of the chapter verifies Jesus' love for them. Can't you just picture Him turning to the city and holding out His hand? Maybe even with tears running down His cheeks? In spite of what He had just said, He summed up God's heart in these last three verses.

About forty years later, the Romans destroyed Jerusalem and slaughtered hundreds of thousands of Jews.[a] This would seem to be a direct fulfillment of the last part of this chapter.

---

[a] Josephus claims that 1.1 million Jews perished in the battle and another 97,000 were enslaved. This doesn't seem quite credible, since only about 20,000 people lived in Jerusalem at the time, and perhaps another million or so in Palestine. However, many people were in Jerusalem for the Passover festivities, and probably some fled there for safety as well. Only God knows the true number, but it was a terrible time.

To Think About

1. Most people do not like hypocrites. But it seems even worse when people who claim to follow God are hypocrites. Why is this true?

2. How can you avoid becoming like the scribes and Pharisees?

3. In the Jewish Bible, the first person to be killed was Abel. The last one was Zachariah. So Jesus was saying here that the scribes and Pharisees would be held responsible for the blood of all the righteous people in the Old Testament. Was this fair? Why?

Lord, keep me from the sin of hypocrisy. Help me not to discredit your name by the life I live.

JESUS IS ... a King who will not tolerate hypocrisy.

DAY 24

Who Is Jesus?

Thus says the LORD of hosts: Zion shall be plowed
like a field, Jerusalem shall become heaps of ruins,
and the mountain of the temple like the bare hills of
the forest. Jeremiah 26:18, NKJV

READ MATTHEW 24

Jesus Foretells Destruction of the Temple

¹ Jesus went out from the temple, and was going on his way. His disciples came
to him to show him the buildings of the temple.

² But he answered them, "You see all of these things, don't you? Most certainly I
tell you, there will not be left here one stone on another, that will not be thrown down."

Signs of the End of the Age

³ As he sat on the Mount of Olives, the disciples came to him privately, saying,
"Tell us, when will these things be? What is the sign of your coming, and of the
end of the age?"

⁴ Jesus answered them, "Be careful that no one leads you astray.

⁵ For many will come in my name, saying, 'I am the Christ,' and will lead many astray.

⁶ You will hear of wars and rumors of wars. See that you aren't troubled, for all this must happen, but the end is not yet.

⁷ For nation will rise against nation, and kingdom against kingdom; and there will be famines, plagues, and earthquakes in various places.

⁸ But all these things are the beginning of birth pains.

⁹ Then they will deliver you up to oppression, and will kill you. You will be hated by all of the nations for my name's sake.

¹⁰ Then many will stumble, and will deliver up one another, and will hate one another.

¹¹ Many false prophets will arise, and will lead many astray.

¹² Because iniquity will be multiplied, the love of many will grow cold.

¹³ But he who endures to the end, the same will be saved.

¹⁴ This Good News of the Kingdom will be preached in the whole world for a testimony to all the nations, and then the end will come.

The Abomination of Desolation

¹⁵ "When, therefore, you see the abomination of desolation, which was spoken of through Daniel the prophet, standing in the holy place (let the reader understand),

¹⁶ then let those who are in Judea flee to the mountains.

¹⁷ Let him who is on the housetop not go down to take out the things that are in his house.

¹⁸ Let him who is in the field not return back to get his clothes.

¹⁹ But woe to those who are with child and to nursing mothers in those days!

²⁰ Pray that your flight will not be in the winter, nor on a Sabbath,

²¹ for then there will be great oppression, such as has not been from the beginning of the world until now, no, nor ever will be.

²² Unless those days had been shortened, no flesh would have been saved. But for the sake of the chosen ones, those days will be shortened.

²³ "Then if any man tells you, 'Behold, here is the Christ,' or, 'There,' don't believe it.

²⁴ For there will arise false christs, and false prophets, and they will show

great signs and wonders, so as to lead astray, if possible, even the chosen ones.

²⁵ "Behold, I have told you beforehand.

²⁶ If therefore they tell you, 'Behold, he is in the wilderness,' don't go out; 'Behold, he is in the inner rooms,' don't believe it.

²⁷ For as the lightning flashes from the east, and is seen even to the west, so will be the coming of the Son of Man.

²⁸ For wherever the carcass is, that is where the vultures gather together.

The Coming of the Son of Man

²⁹ But immediately after the oppression of those days, the sun will be darkened, the moon will not give its light, the stars will fall from the sky, and the powers of the heavens will be shaken;

³⁰ and then the sign of the Son of Man will appear in the sky. Then all the tribes of the earth will mourn, and they will see the Son of Man coming on the clouds of the sky with power and great glory.

³¹ He will send out his angels with a great sound of a trumpet, and they will gather together his chosen ones from the four winds, from one end of the sky to the other.

The Lesson of the Fig Tree

³² "Now from the fig tree learn this parable. When its branch has now become tender, and produces its leaves, you know that the summer is near.

³³ Even so you also, when you see all these things, know that it is near, even at the doors.

³⁴ Most certainly I tell you, this generation will not pass away, until all these things are accomplished.

³⁵ Heaven and earth will pass away, but my words will not pass away.

No One Knows That Day and Hour

³⁶ But no one knows of that day and hour, not even the angels of heaven, but my Father only.

³⁷ "As the days of Noah were, so will be the coming of the Son of Man.

³⁸ For as in those days which were before the flood they were eating and drinking, marrying and giving in marriage, until the day that Noah entered into the ship,

^{39} and they didn't know until the flood came, and took them all away, so will be the coming of the Son of Man.

^{40} Then two men will be in the field: one will be taken and one will be left.

^{41} Two women will be grinding at the mill: one will be taken and one will be left.

^{42} Watch therefore, for you don't know in what hour your Lord comes.

^{43} But know this, that if the master of the house had known in what watch of the night the thief was coming, he would have watched, and would not have allowed his house to be broken into.

^{44} Therefore also be ready, for in an hour that you don't expect, the Son of Man will come.

^{45} "Who then is the faithful and wise servant, whom his lord has set over his household, to give them their food in due season?

^{46} Blessed is that servant whom his lord finds doing so when he comes.

^{47} Most certainly I tell you that he will set him over all that he has.

^{48} But if that evil servant should say in his heart, 'My lord is delaying his coming,'

^{49} and begins to beat his fellow servants, and eat and drink with the drunkards,

^{50} the lord of that servant will come in a day when he doesn't expect it, and in an hour when he doesn't know it,

^{51} and will cut him in pieces, and appoint his portion with the hypocrites. That is where the weeping and grinding of teeth will be.

Who Is Jesus?

Bible scholars have interpreted this chapter in several ways. Some put it in the past, at the destruction of Jerusalem. Some put it in the future, at some future disaster. Still others feel that it may apply to both, and have a dual fulfillment.

More important than figuring out all the details is noticing that life in this world will not go on forever as it is now. We know that some of the things Jesus talked about have already been fulfilled; we know that the temple was destroyed. We

don't know what the future holds, but we know that someday our King, Jesus, will return to claim His people.

You will notice a few other things. Life on earth will often be difficult for Christians. Many will give up when the going gets tough.
And lastly, no matter what modern-day prophets may claim,
none of us knows when the end will be. People have often set
a date for the end of the world. But these have all been wrong.

Date setting is a sure sign of a false prophet. Don't be deceived.
Just be ready at all times, and you won't need to worry about it.

To Think About

1. If you are interested in seeing more details about this
   chapter from another perspective, read Luke 21.

2. In what ways will the return of Jesus be like the times
   of Noah?

3. Do we need to be afraid of the end of the world or the
   return of Jesus? Explain your answer.

4. Are you ready for Jesus' return?

*Lord, I pray that I would not give up if in following you
the going gets tough. Help me to look for your return
and be ready and waiting when you come.*

JESUS IS ... a King who
will return to rescue His people
from the evil of this world.

DAY 25

Who Is Jesus?

At that time Michael shall stand up, the great prince who
stands watch over the sons of your people; and there shall
be a time of trouble, such as never was since there was
a nation, even to that time. And at that time your people
shall be delivered, every one who is found written in the
book. And many of those who sleep in the dust of the earth
shall awake, some to everlasting life, some to shame and
everlasting contempt. Daniel 12:1–2, NKJV

READ MATTHEW 25

The Parable of the Ten Virgins

¹ "Then the Kingdom of Heaven will be like ten virgins, who took their
lamps, and went out to meet the bridegroom.

² Five of them were foolish, and five were wise.

³ Those who were foolish, when they took their lamps, took no oil with them,

⁴ but the wise took oil in their vessels with their lamps.

⁵ Now while the bridegroom delayed, they all slumbered and slept.

⁶ But at midnight there was a cry, 'Behold! The bridegroom is coming!
Come out to meet him!'

⁷ Then all those virgins arose, and trimmed their lamps.

⁸ The foolish said to the wise, 'Give us some of your oil, for our lamps are going out.'

⁹ But the wise answered, saying, 'What if there isn't enough for us and you? You go rather to those who sell, and buy for yourselves.'

¹⁰ While they went away to buy, the bridegroom came, and those who were ready went in with him to the marriage feast, and the door was shut.

¹¹ Afterward the other virgins also came, saying, 'Lord, Lord, open to us.'

¹² But he answered, 'Most certainly I tell you, I don't know you.'

¹³ Watch therefore, for you don't know the day nor the hour in which the Son of Man is coming.

The Parable of the Talents

¹⁴ "For it is like a man, going into another country, who called his own servants, and entrusted his goods to them.

¹⁵ To one he gave five talents, to another two, to another one; to each according to his own ability. Then he went on his journey.

¹⁶ Immediately he who received the five talents went and traded with them, and made another five talents.

¹⁷ In the same way, he also who got the two gained another two.

¹⁸ But he who received the one talent went away and dug in the earth, and hid his lord's money.

¹⁹ "Now after a long time the lord of those servants came, and reconciled accounts with them.

²⁰ He who received the five talents came and brought another five talents, saying, 'Lord, you delivered to me five talents. Behold, I have gained another five talents in addition to them.'

²¹ "His lord said to him, 'Well done, good and faithful servant. You have been faithful over a few things, I will set you over many things. Enter into the joy of your lord.'

²² "He also who got the two talents came and said, 'Lord, you delivered to me two talents. Behold, I have gained another two talents in addition to them.'

²³ "His lord said to him, 'Well done, good and faithful servant. You have been faithful over a few things, I will set you over many things. Enter into the joy of your lord.'

²⁴ "He also who had received the one talent came and said, 'Lord, I knew you that you are a hard man, reaping where you didn't sow, and gathering where you didn't scatter.

²⁵ I was afraid, and went away and hid your talent in the earth. Behold, you have what is yours.'

²⁶ "But his lord answered him, 'You wicked and slothful servant. You knew that I reap where I didn't sow, and gather where I didn't scatter.

²⁷ You ought therefore to have deposited my money with the bankers, and at my coming I should have received back my own with interest.

²⁸ Take away therefore the talent from him, and give it to him who has the ten talents.

²⁹ For to everyone who has will be given, and he will have abundance, but from him who doesn't have, even that which he has will be taken away.

³⁰ Throw out the unprofitable servant into the outer darkness, where there will be weeping and gnashing of teeth.'

The Final Judgment

³¹ "But when the Son of Man comes in his glory, and all the holy angels with him, then he will sit on the throne of his glory.

³² Before him all the nations will be gathered, and he will separate them one from another, as a shepherd separates the sheep from the goats.

³³ He will set the sheep on his right hand, but the goats on the left.

³⁴ Then the King will tell those on his right hand, 'Come, blessed of my Father, inherit the Kingdom prepared for you from the foundation of the world;

^{35} for I was hungry, and you gave me food to eat. I was thirsty, and you gave me drink. I was a stranger, and you took me in.

^{36} I was naked, and you clothed me. I was sick, and you visited me. I was in prison, and you came to me.'

^{37} "Then the righteous will answer him, saying, 'Lord, when did we see you hungry, and feed you; or thirsty, and give you a drink?

^{38} When did we see you as a stranger, and take you in; or naked, and clothe you?

^{39} When did we see you sick, or in prison, and come to you?'

^{40} "The King will answer them, 'Most certainly I tell you, because you did it to one of the least of these my brothers, you did it to me.'

^{41} Then he will say also to those on the left hand, 'Depart from me, you cursed, into the eternal fire which is prepared for the devil and his angels;

^{42} for I was hungry, and you didn't give me food to eat; I was thirsty, and you gave me no drink;

^{43} I was a stranger, and you didn't take me in; naked, and you didn't clothe me; sick, and in prison, and you didn't visit me.'

^{44} "Then they will also answer, saying, 'Lord, when did we see you hungry, or thirsty, or a stranger, or naked, or sick, or in prison, and didn't help you?'

^{45} "Then he will answer them, saying, 'Most certainly I tell you, because you didn't do it to one of the least of these, you didn't do it to me.'

^{46} These will go away into eternal punishment, but the righteous into eternal life."

Who Is Jesus?

This chapter continues Jesus' discourse from the last chapter. The first two sections are parables which warn us to be ready for Jesus' return. These two stories teach us that not everyone who claims to be part of His kingdom will be ready to meet Him.

In the parable of the ten virgins, very likely you would not have noticed any difference between them. Yet half of them were not ready when the bridegroom came. None of them realized this until it was too late to make the necessary preparations to meet Him. They ended up outside in the darkness, the door shut in their faces.

The parable of the talents gives a similar warning. Notice that the servants weren't judged by the results of their work. Rather, they were judged by the effort they put into it and their faithfulness to their master.

In the last part of the chapter, Jesus talked about the final judgment. He pictured all the people who had ever lived gathered before Him. Notice what He judged them by:

- I was hungry and you gave me food.
- I was thirsty and you gave me something to drink.
- I was a stranger and you welcomed me.
- I needed clothing and you gave me some.
- I was sick and you visited me.
- I was in prison and you visited me.

None of the people he was talking to remembered doing these things. And none of the people on the other side remembered NOT doing them. Jesus clarified this by telling the disciples that when they did such things, they were doing it for Him. When they didn't do them, they were rejecting Him.

To Think About

1. In what ways might you be like one of the foolish virgins? How might you be like one of the wise?

2. Which servant in the parable of the talents are you like?

3. Does Jesus' story of the last judgment tell us that as long as we do good things to other people, we will be saved? You might want to read Matthew 7:21-23, and Revelation 20:11-15 for more details before deciding.

Father, help me to serve you. I know I cannot earn my way to heaven, but I want to do what I can to help those in need around me.

JESUS IS...
a King who will judge the world someday.

DAY 26

Who Is Jesus?

Awake, O sword, against My Shepherd, against the Man
who is My Companion, says the LORD of hosts. Strike the
Shepherd, and the sheep will be scattered; then I will turn
My hand against the little ones. Zechariah 13:7, NKJV

Introduction

This is the beginning of the last section of Matthew. For the
disciples this seemed like the end. They could not understand
what was happening, even though Jesus had tried many times
to explain it to them. Pay careful attention to these last chapters because they tell us about the most important event in
human history, past or future.

The Plot to Kill Jesus

[1] When Jesus had finished all these words, he said to his disciples, .

[2] "You know that after two days the Passover is coming, and the Son of Man will be delivered up to be crucified."

[3] Then the chief priests, the scribes, and the elders of the people were gathered together in the court of the high priest, who was called Caiaphas.

[4] They took counsel together that they might take Jesus by deceit, and kill him.

[5] But they said, "Not during the feast, lest a riot occur among the people."

Jesus Anointed at Bethany

[6] Now when Jesus was in Bethany, in the house of Simon the leper,

[7] a woman came to him having an alabaster jar of very expensive ointment, and she poured it on his head as he sat at the table.

[8] But when his disciples saw this, they were indignant, saying, "Why this waste?

[9] For this ointment might have been sold for much, and given to the poor."

[10] However, knowing this, Jesus said to them, "Why do you trouble the woman? She has done a good work for me.

[11] For you always have the poor with you; but you don't always have me.

[12] For in pouring this ointment on my body, she did it to prepare me for burial.

[13] Most certainly I tell you, wherever this Good News is preached in the whole world, what this woman has done will also be spoken of as a memorial of her."

Judas to Betray Jesus

[14] Then one of the twelve, who was called Judas Iscariot, went to the chief priests,

[15] and said, "What are you willing to give me, that I should deliver him to you?" They weighed out for him thirty pieces of silver.

[16] From that time he sought opportunity to betray him.

The Passover with the Disciples

[17] Now on the first day of unleavened bread, the disciples came to Jesus, saying to him, "Where do you want us to prepare for you to eat the Passover?"

¹⁸ He said, "Go into the city to a certain person, and tell him, 'The Teacher says, "My time is at hand. I will keep the Passover at your house with my disciples." ' "

¹⁹ The disciples did as Jesus commanded them, and they prepared the Passover.

²⁰ Now when evening had come, he was reclining at the table with the twelve disciples.

²¹ As they were eating, he said, "Most certainly I tell you that one of you will betray me."

²² They were exceedingly sorrowful, and each began to ask him, "It isn't me, is it, Lord?"

²³ He answered, "He who dipped his hand with me in the dish, the same will betray me.

²⁴ The Son of Man goes, even as it is written of him, but woe to that man through whom the Son of Man is betrayed! It would be better for that man if he had not been born."

²⁵ Judas, who betrayed him, answered, "It isn't me, is it, Rabbi?" He said to him, "You said it."

Institution of the Lord's Supper

²⁶ As they were eating, Jesus took bread, gave thanks for it, and broke it. He gave to the disciples, and said, "Take, eat; this is my body."

²⁷ He took the cup, gave thanks, and gave to them, saying, "All of you drink it,

²⁸ for this is my blood of the new covenant, which is poured out for many for the remission of sins.

²⁹ But I tell you that I will not drink of this fruit of the vine from now on, until that day when I drink it anew with you in my Father's Kingdom."

Jesus Foretells Peter's Denial

³⁰ When they had sung a hymn, they went out to the Mount of Olives.

³¹ Then Jesus said to them, "All of you will be made to stumble because of me tonight, for it is written, 'I will strike the shepherd, and the sheep of the flock will be scattered.'

³² But after I am raised up, I will go before you into Galilee."

³³ But Peter answered him, "Even if all will be made to stumble because of you, I will never be made to stumble."

³⁴ Jesus said to him, "Most certainly I tell you that tonight, before the rooster crows, you will deny me three times."

³⁵ Peter said to him, "Even if I must die with you, I will not deny you." All of the disciples also said likewise.

Jesus Prays in Gethsemane

³⁶ Then Jesus came with them to a place called Gethsemane, and said to his disciples, "Sit here, while I go there and pray."

³⁷ He took with him Peter and the two sons of Zebedee, and began to be sorrowful and severely troubled.

³⁸ Then he said to them, "My soul is exceedingly sorrowful, even to death. Stay here, and watch with me."

³⁹ He went forward a little, fell on his face, and prayed, saying, "My Father, if it is possible, let this cup pass away from me; nevertheless, not what I desire, but what you desire."

⁴⁰ He came to the disciples, and found them sleeping, and said to Peter, "What, couldn't you watch with me for one hour?

⁴¹ Watch and pray, that you don't enter into temptation. The spirit indeed is willing, but the flesh is weak."

⁴² Again, a second time he went away, and prayed, saying, "My Father, if this cup can't pass away from me unless I drink it, your desire be done."

⁴³ He came again and found them sleeping, for their eyes were heavy.

⁴⁴ He left them again, went away, and prayed a third time, saying the same words.

⁴⁵ Then he came to his disciples, and said to them, "Sleep on now, and take your rest. Behold, the hour is at hand, and the Son of Man is betrayed into the hands of sinners.

⁴⁶ Arise, let's be going. Behold, he who betrays me is at hand."

Betrayal and Arrest of Jesus

⁴⁷ While he was still speaking, behold, Judas, one of the twelve, came, and with

him a great multitude with swords and clubs, from the chief priests and elders of the people.

[48] Now he who betrayed him gave them a sign, saying, "Whoever I kiss, he is the one. Seize him."

[49] Immediately he came to Jesus, and said, "Hail, Rabbi!" and kissed him.

[50] Jesus said to him, "Friend, why are you here?" Then they came and laid hands on Jesus, and took him.

[51] Behold, one of those who were with Jesus stretched out his hand, and drew his sword, and struck the servant of the high priest, and struck off his ear.

[52] Then Jesus said to him, "Put your sword back into its place, for all those who take the sword will die by the sword.

[53] Or do you think that I couldn't ask my Father, and he would even now send me more than twelve legions of angels?

[54] How then would the Scriptures be fulfilled that it must be so?"

[55] In that hour Jesus said to the multitudes, "Have you come out as against a robber with swords and clubs to seize me? I sat daily in the temple teaching, and you didn't arrest me.

[56] But all this has happened, that the Scriptures of the prophets might be fulfilled." Then all the disciples left him, and fled.

Jesus Before Caiaphas and the Council

[57] Those who had taken Jesus led him away to Caiaphas the high priest, where the scribes and the elders were gathered together.

[58] But Peter followed him from a distance, to the court of the high priest, and entered in and sat with the officers, to see the end.

[59] Now the chief priests, the elders, and the whole council sought false testimony against Jesus, that they might put him to death;

[60] and they found none. Even though many false witnesses came forward, they found none. But at last two false witnesses came forward,

[61] and said, "This man said, 'I am able to destroy the temple of God, and to build it in three days.'"

[62] The high priest stood up, and said to him, "Have you no answer? What is this

that these testify against you?"

⁶³ But Jesus held his peace. The high priest answered him, "I adjure you by the living God, that you tell us whether you are the Christ, the Son of God."

⁶⁴ Jesus said to him, "You have said it. Nevertheless, I tell you, after this you will see the Son of Man sitting at the right hand of Power, and coming on the clouds of the sky."

⁶⁵ Then the high priest tore his clothing, saying, "He has spoken blasphemy! Why do we need any more witnesses? Behold, now you have heard his blasphemy.

⁶⁶ What do you think?" They answered, "He is worthy of death!"

⁶⁷ Then they spat in his face and beat him with their fists, and some slapped him,

⁶⁸ saying, "Prophesy to us, you Christ! Who hit you?"

Peter Denies Jesus

⁶⁹ Now Peter was sitting outside in the court, and a maid came to him, saying, "You were also with Jesus, the Galilean!"

⁷⁰ But he denied it before them all, saying, "I don't know what you are talking about."

⁷¹ When he had gone out onto the porch, someone else saw him, and said to those who were there, "This man also was with Jesus of Nazareth."

⁷² Again he denied it with an oath, "I don't know the man."

⁷³ After a little while those who stood by came and said to Peter, "Surely you are also one of them, for your speech makes you known."

⁷⁴ Then he began to curse and to swear, "I don't know the man!" Immediately the rooster crowed.

⁷⁵ Peter remembered the word which Jesus had said to him, "Before the rooster crows, you will deny me three times." He went out and wept bitterly.

Who Is Jesus?

This is the longest chapter in Matthew. At the beginning, Jesus again warned His disciples that His death was close. This time it was only two days away. The disciples didn't understand. They could not believe that their dreams would end like this, in one big crash, with the death of their King and Master.

It started with an official meeting led by the high priest himself.

In the meantime, Jesus was at a gathering in Bethany, a small town close to Jerusalem. Here a woman anointed Jesus. The disciples looked at this as being very wasteful, but Jesus knew her heart and defended her for what she did. This waste of valuable perfume was the last straw for Judas, who would have preferred to sell it, possibly so he could steal the money. He went back to Jerusalem, where he offered to betray Jesus.

Jesus ate the Passover feast with His disciples either that evening or the next evening, then departed to the Mount of Olives to spend the night. Here He prayed, all alone, while His disciples slept close by. A bit later, after Jesus had awakened the disciples, Judas and his band of rabble-rousers arrived to arrest Him. They took Him away while the disciples—His best friends—ran for their lives.

This mob took Jesus to the high priest where they held a fake trial, which was illegal according to the law they claimed to uphold. They mocked Him, hit Him, and spit in His face.

In the meantime, Peter came slinking in the side door to see what was happening. Peter would have considered himself Jesus' best friend. He had vowed that He would die with Jesus if necessary. But Peter miserably failed the test and even denied that he knew Jesus.

To Think About

1.   Read this chapter carefully and try to see into the heart

of Jesus. Can you see how He tried to reach out to the disciples, His closest friends? Can you see their lack of understanding of His need? He ended up facing this greatest test of His life all by Himself. What does this show you about His ability to love?

2. Why do you think the Jewish leaders hated Jesus so much that they would stoop to acting like this to get rid of Him?

3. Why were the priests unable to put together a case against Jesus, even with the witnesses they called? How did they finally manage to come up with a sentence of death?

4. Remember, Jesus was God. He could have walked away from these people. He could have destroyed them with a wave of His hand. Why didn't He?

Lord, I know you went through all this suffering for me. All I can do is humbly say, "Thank you."

JESUS IS ... a King who understands what we need and cares about us.

DAY 27

Who Is Jesus?

The Lord GOD has opened My ear; and I was not rebellious, nor did I turn away. I gave My back to those who struck Me, and My cheeks to those who plucked out the beard; I did not hide My face from shame and spitting. Isaiah 50:5–6, NKJV

READ MATTHEW 27

Jesus Delivered to Pilate

¹ Now when morning had come, all the chief priests and the elders of the people took counsel against Jesus to put him to death:

² and they bound him, and led him away, and delivered him up to Pontius Pilate, the governor.

Judas Hangs Himself

³ Then Judas, who betrayed him, when he saw that Jesus was condemned, felt remorse, and brought back the thirty pieces of silver to the chief priests and elders,

⁴ saying, "I have sinned in that I betrayed innocent blood." But they said, "What

is that to us? You see to it."

⁵ He threw down the pieces of silver in the sanctuary, and departed. He went away and hanged himself.

⁶ The chief priests took the pieces of silver, and said, "It's not lawful to put them into the treasury, since it is the price of blood."

⁷ They took counsel, and bought the potter's field with them, to bury strangers in.

⁸ Therefore that field was called "The Field of Blood" to this day.

⁹ Then that which was spoken through Jeremiah the prophet was fulfilled, saying, "They took the thirty pieces of silver, the price of him upon whom a price had been set, whom some of the children of Israel priced,

¹⁰ and they gave them for the potter's field, as the Lord commanded me."

Jesus Before Pilate

¹¹ Now Jesus stood before the governor: and the governor asked him, saying, "Are you the King of the Jews?" Jesus said to him, "So you say."

¹² When he was accused by the chief priests and elders, he answered nothing.

¹³ Then Pilate said to him, "Don't you hear how many things they testify against you?"

¹⁴ He gave him no answer, not even one word, so that the governor marveled greatly.

The Crowd Chooses Barabbas

¹⁵ Now at the feast the governor was accustomed to release to the multitude one prisoner, whom they desired.

¹⁶ They had then a notable prisoner, called Barabbas.

¹⁷ When therefore they were gathered together, Pilate said to them, "Whom do you want me to release to you? Barabbas, or Jesus, who is called Christ?"

¹⁸ For he knew that because of envy they had delivered him up.

¹⁹ While he was sitting on the judgment seat, his wife sent to him, saying, "Have nothing to do with that righteous man, for I have suffered many things today in a dream because of him."

²⁰ Now the chief priests and the elders persuaded the multitudes to ask for

Barabbas, and destroy Jesus.

²¹ But the governor answered them, "Which of the two do you want me to release to you?" They said, "Barabbas!"

²² Pilate said to them, "What then shall I do to Jesus, who is called Christ?" They all said to him, "Let him be crucified!"

²³ But the governor said, "Why? What evil has he done?" But they cried out exceedingly, saying, "Let him be crucified!"

Pilate Delivers Jesus to Be Crucified

²⁴ So when Pilate saw that nothing was being gained, but rather that a disturbance was starting, he took water, and washed his hands before the multitude, saying, "I am innocent of the blood of this righteous person. You see to it."

²⁵ All the people answered, "May his blood be on us, and on our children!"

²⁶ Then he released to them Barabbas, but Jesus he flogged and delivered to be crucified.

Jesus Is Mocked

²⁷ Then the governor's soldiers took Jesus into the Praetorium, and gathered the whole garrison together against him.

²⁸ They stripped him, and put a scarlet robe on him.

²⁹ They braided a crown of thorns and put it on his head, and a reed in his right hand; and they kneeled down before him, and mocked him, saying, "Hail, King of the Jews!"

³⁰ They spat on him, and took the reed and struck him on the head.

³¹ When they had mocked him, they took the robe off him, and put his clothes on him, and led him away to crucify him.

The Crucifixion

³² As they came out, they found a man of Cyrene, Simon by name, and they compelled him to go with them, that he might carry his cross.

³³ When they came to a place called "Golgotha," that is to say, "The place of a skull,"

³⁴ they gave him sour wine to drink mixed with gall. When he had tasted it, he would not drink.

³⁵ When they had crucified him, they divided his clothing among them, casting lots,

³⁶ and they sat and watched him there.

³⁷ They set up over his head the accusation against him written, "THIS IS JESUS, THE KING OF THE JEWS."

³⁸ Then there were two robbers crucified with him, one on his right hand and one on the left.

³⁹ Those who passed by blasphemed him, wagging their heads,

⁴⁰ and saying, "You who destroy the temple, and build it in three days, save yourself! If you are the Son of God, come down from the cross!"

⁴¹ Likewise the chief priests also mocking, with the scribes, the Pharisees, and the elders, said,

⁴² "He saved others, but he can't save himself. If he is the King of Israel, let him come down from the cross now, and we will believe in him.

⁴³ He trusts in God. Let God deliver him now, if he wants him; for he said, 'I am the Son of God.' "

⁴⁴ The robbers also who were crucified with him cast on him the same reproach.

The Death of Jesus

⁴⁵ Now from the sixth hour there was darkness over all the land until the ninth hour.

⁴⁶ About the ninth hour Jesus cried with a loud voice, saying, "Eli, Eli, lima sabachthani?" That is, "My God, my God, why have you forsaken me?"

⁴⁷ Some of them who stood there, when they heard it, said, "This man is calling Elijah."

⁴⁸ Immediately one of them ran, and took a sponge, and filled it with vinegar, and put it on a reed, and gave him a drink.

⁴⁹ The rest said, "Let him be. Let's see whether Elijah comes to save him."

⁵⁰ Jesus cried again with a loud voice, and yielded up his spirit.

⁵¹ Behold, the veil of the temple was torn in two from the top to the bottom. The earth quaked and the rocks were split.

⁵² The tombs were opened, and many bodies of the saints who had fallen asleep were raised;

⁵³ and coming out of the tombs after his resurrection, they entered into the holy city and appeared to many.

⁵⁴ Now the centurion, and those who were with him watching Jesus, when they saw the earthquake, and the things that were done, feared exceedingly, saying, "Truly this was the Son of God."

⁵⁵ Many women were there watching from afar, who had followed Jesus from Galilee, serving him.

⁵⁶ Among them were Mary Magdalene, Mary the mother of James and Joses, and the mother of the sons of Zebedee.

Jesus Is Buried

⁵⁷ When evening had come, a rich man from Arimathaea, named Joseph, who himself was also Jesus' disciple came.

⁵⁸ This man went to Pilate, and asked for Jesus' body. Then Pilate commanded the body to be given up.

⁵⁹ Joseph took the body, and wrapped it in a clean linen cloth,

⁶⁰ and laid it in his own new tomb, which he had cut out in the rock, and he rolled a great stone against the door of the tomb, and departed.

⁶¹ Mary Magdalene was there, and the other Mary, sitting opposite the tomb.

The Guard at the Tomb

⁶² Now on the next day, which was the day after the Preparation Day, the chief priests and the Pharisees were gathered together to Pilate,

⁶³ saying, "Sir, we remember what that deceiver said while he was still alive: 'After three days I will rise again.'

⁶⁴ Command therefore that the tomb be made secure until the third day, lest perhaps his disciples come at night and steal him away, and tell the people, 'He is risen from the dead;' and the last deception will be worse than the first."

⁶⁵ Pilate said to them, "You have a guard. Go, make it as secure as you can."

⁶⁶ So they went with the guard and made the tomb secure, sealing the stone.

Who Is Jesus?

The Romans did not allow the Jews to carry out a death sentence, so the Jews needed to take Jesus to Pilate, the Roman governor at the time.

In the meantime, Judas saw the results of what he had done. Had he expected that Jesus would escape as He had many times before? Evidently he either did not expect what happened, or he felt remorse when it did happen. Either way, his guilt overwhelmed him, and he committed suicide.

Pilate's trial of Jesus was a farce. He knew that if he didn't let the Jewish leaders have their way, he would face a serious uprising. In Pilate's mind, the life of an itinerant street preacher wasn't important enough for him to jeopardize his position. He therefore washed his hands of the situation and let them have their way.

Matthew doesn't go into depth in describing everything that happened. But if you try to put yourself into Jesus' shoes as you read the last half of the chapter, it will make it more real to you. The mockery, the scourging, the crown of thorns, and the purple robe all tell us what kind of man, or King, Jesus was. Imagine God watching this. Or the angels.

Apparently Jesus was too weak to carry His cross. Someone else had to do it for Him. The last verses show us the paradox of human beings nailing Jesus to a cross and letting Him die.

The One who had earlier said He had no place to lay His head had to be buried in a borrowed tomb.

To Think About

1. The thought of men putting a person like Jesus to death is hard to understand. Jesus was God. He healed the sick and brought dead people back to life. He fed large multitudes with a small amount of food and walked on the water. He cast out demons and defeated the devil himself. How could people put a man like this to death?

2. Do you think Pilate understood what was really going on?

3. One of the most heart-wrenching statements in this chapter is in verse 46, where Jesus cried out, "MY GOD, MY GOD, WHY HAVE YOU FORSAKEN ME?" Do you think God really forsook Jesus? Or was this His humanity crying out?

Lord, help me to understand what you did for me, and that you suffered so I could be delivered from my sin.

JESUS IS . . . a King who was not afraid to die for His people.

DAY 28

Who Is Jesus?

Who has declared this from ancient time? Who has told it from that time? Have not I, the LORD? And there is no other God besides Me, a just God and a Savior; there is none besides Me. Look to Me, and be saved, all you ends of the earth! For I am God, and there is no other. Isaiah 45:21–22, NKJV

READ MATTHEW 28

The Resurrection

¹ Now after the Sabbath, as it began to dawn on the first day of the week, Mary Magdalene and the other Mary came to see the tomb.

² Behold, there was a great earthquake, for an angel of the Lord descended from the sky, and came and rolled away the stone from the door, and sat on it.

³ His appearance was like lightning, and his clothing white as snow.

⁴ For fear of him, the guards shook, and became like dead men.

⁵ The angel answered the women, "Don't be afraid, for I know that you seek Jesus, who has been crucified.

^{6} He is not here, for he has risen, just like he said. Come, see the place where the Lord was lying.

^{7} Go quickly and tell his disciples, 'He has risen from the dead, and behold, he goes before you into Galilee; there you will see him.' Behold, I have told you."

^{8} They departed quickly from the tomb with fear and great joy, and ran to bring his disciples word.

^{9} As they went to tell his disciples, behold, Jesus met them, saying, "Rejoice!" They came and took hold of his feet, and worshiped him.

^{10} Then Jesus said to them, "Don't be afraid. Go tell my brothers that they should go into Galilee, and there they will see me."

The Report of the Guard

^{11} Now while they were going, behold, some of the guards came into the city, and told the chief priests all the things that had happened.

^{12} When they were assembled with the elders, and had taken counsel, they gave a large amount of silver to the soldiers,

^{13} saying, "Say that his disciples came by night, and stole him away while we slept.

^{14} If this comes to the governor's ears, we will persuade him and make you free of worry."

^{15} So they took the money and did as they were told. This saying was spread abroad among the Jews, and continues until today.

The Great Commission

^{16} But the eleven disciples went into Galilee, to the mountain where Jesus had sent them.

^{17} When they saw him, they bowed down to him, but some doubted.

^{18} Jesus came to them and spoke to them, saying, "All authority has been given to me in heaven and on earth.

^{19} Go and make disciples of all nations, baptizing them in the name of the Father and of the Son and of the Holy Spirit,

^{20} teaching them to observe all things that I commanded you. Behold, I am with you always, even to the end of the age." Amen.

Who Is Jesus?

Jesus may have been crucified on Thursday or on Friday. The Bible isn't totally clear on this point. But on the Sabbath day everyone rested. The disciples probably gathered in seclusion somewhere, afraid that the Jewish leaders would be after them as well.

Then came Sunday morning.

If you have been reading the Book of Matthew carefully, it will not really surprise you that no grave could hold Jesus very long. How could you keep the Son of God in a tomb? It would take much more than a Roman seal and a group of soldiers to accomplish that. When Jesus arose, the men who cowered in abject terror on the ground in front of the tomb knew that it had been no ordinary man they had been guarding.

It was all over—finished. The pain and the mockery were behind Him. Jesus' work was done, but the disciples' part was only beginning. Their challenge was to spread the Good News, the Gospel of the kingdom, far and wide.

That is still our challenge today.

To Think About

1. As you read the various versions of this account in the Gospels, you can't help but notice that it was the women who went to the tomb. It was also the women who saw Jesus first. The men stayed huddled in hiding. Why do you think this was the case?

2. The word *Gospel* means good news. In what ways is the story of Jesus good news?

3. Take some time to think about Jesus and what you have learned about Him from the Gospel of Matthew. Has His story done anything for you? If so, what?

Lord, thank you. Thank you for dying, and thank you for living. I am not worthy of your sacrifice for me, but I want to serve you and tell others the Good News.

JESUS IS ... a King who is worthy of our worship!

About the Author

Lester Bauman was born into an Old Order Mennonite home close to Kitchener, Ontario. Later his family joined a local conservative Mennonite church. As a young-married man, he taught for five years in several Christian schools. Later he worked for thirteen years out of a home office for Rod and Staff Publishers, Inc. as a writer and editor. During this time, he and his wife Marlene moved with their family from Ontario to Alberta, where they live presently. They have six children and eleven grandchildren, and are members of a local Western Fellowship Mennonite Church.

During his time with Rod and Staff, Lester wrote ten books, including *The True Christian* and *God and Uncle Dale,* both available from Christian Aid Ministries. He spent a number of years in Alberta working as an HR manager in a corporate setting. He now works for the Christian Aid Ministries billboard evangelism ministry out of a home office, doing content writing for their website, answering correspondence, and writing resource materials.

Lester has written several other books published by Christian Aid Ministries: *Sylvester's Journal* and *What Is the Bible?* He is also working on several other books as time allows.

You can contact Lester through his personal website at www.lbauman.ca or by email at lester.bauman@gmail.com. You may also write to him in care of Christian Aid Ministries, P.O. Box 360, Berlin, Ohio 44610.

About Christian Aid Ministries

Christian Aid Ministries was founded in 1981 as a nonprofit, tax-exempt 501(c)(3) organization. Its primary purpose is to provide a trustworthy and efficient channel for Amish, Mennonite, and other conservative Anabaptist groups and individuals to minister to physical and spiritual needs around the world. This is in response to the command to "... do good unto all men, especially unto them who are of the household of faith" (Galatians 6:10).

Each year, CAM supporters provide 15-20 million pounds

of food, clothing, medicines, seeds, Bibles, Bible story books, and other Christian literature for needy people. Most of the aid goes to orphans and Christian families. Supporters' funds also help to clean up and rebuild for natural disaster victims, put up Gospel billboards in the U.S., support several church-planting efforts, operate two medical clinics, and provide resources for needy families to make their own living. CAM's main purposes for providing aid are to help and encourage God's people and bring the Gospel to a lost and dying world.

CAM has staff, warehouses, and distribution networks in Romania, Moldova, Ukraine, Haiti, Nicaragua, Liberia, Israel, and Kenya. Aside from management, supervisory personnel, and bookkeeping operations, volunteers do most of the work at CAM locations. Each year, volunteers at our warehouses, field bases, Disaster Response Services projects, and other locations donate over 200,000 hours of work.

CAM's ultimate purpose is to glorify God and help enlarge His kingdom. ". . . whatsoever ye do, do all to the glory of God" (1 Corinthians 10:31).

The Way to God and Peace

We live in a world contaminated by sin. Sin is anything that goes against God's holy standards. When we do not follow the guidelines that God our Creator gave us, we are guilty of sin. Sin separates us from God, the source of life.

Since the time when the first man and woman, Adam and Eve, sinned in the Garden of Eden, sin has been universal. The Bible says that we all have "sinned and come short of the glory of God" (Romans 3:23). It also says that the natural consequence for that sin is eternal death, or punishment in an eternal hell: "Then when lust hath conceived, it bringeth forth sin: and sin, when it is finished, bringeth forth death" (James 1:15).

But we do not have to suffer eternal death in hell. God provided forgiveness for our sins through the death of His only Son, Jesus Christ. Because Jesus was perfect and without sin, He could die in our place. "For God so loved the world that he gave his only begotten Son, that whosoever believeth in him should not perish, but have everlasting life" (John 3:16).

A sacrifice is something given to benefit someone else. It costs the giver greatly. Jesus was God's sacrifice. Jesus' death takes away the penalty of sin for all those who accept this sacrifice and truly repent of their sins. To repent of sins means to be truly sorry for and turn away from the things we have done that have violated God's standards (Acts 2:38; 3:19).

Jesus died, but He did not remain dead. After three days, God's Spirit miraculously raised Him to life again. God's Spirit does something similar in us. When we receive Jesus as our sacrifice and repent of our sins, our hearts are changed. We become spiritually alive! We develop new desires and attitudes (2 Corinthians 5:17). We begin to make choices that please God (1 John 3:9). If we do fail and commit sins, we can ask God for forgiveness. "If we confess our sins, he is faithful and just to forgive us our sins, and to cleanse us from all unrighteousness" (1 John 1:9).

Once our hearts have been changed, we want to continue growing spiritually. We will be happy to let Jesus be the Master of our lives and will want to become more like Him. To do this, we must meditate on God's Word and commune with God in prayer. We will testify to others of this change by being baptized and sharing the good news of God's victory over sin and death. Fellowship with a faithful group of believers will strengthen our walk with God (1 John 1:7).

Notes